LITERARY/CULTURAL THEORY

DE CONSTRUCTION
AND
POSTSTRUCTURALISM

Literary/Cultural Theory provides concise and lucid introductions to a range of key concepts and theorists in contemporary literary and cultural theory. Original and contemporary in presentation, and eschewing jargon, each book in the series presents students of humanities and social sciences with exhaustive overviews of theories and theorists, while also introducing them to the mechanics of reading literary/cultural texts using critical tools. Each book also carries glossaries of key terms and ideas, and pointers for further reading and research. Written by scholar-teachers who have taught critical theory for years, and vetted by some of the foremost experts in the field, the series Literary/Cultural Theory is indispensable to students and teachers.

Series Editors

Allen Hibbard
Middle Tennessee State University
Andrew Slade
University of Dayton
Herman Rapaport
Wake Forest University
Imre Szeman
University of Alberta
Krishna Sen
University of Calcutta
Scott Slovic
University of Idaho
Sumit Chakrabarti
Presidency University, Kolkata

Also in the series

Psychoanalytic Theory and Criticism
Feminisms
Jacques Lacan
Dalit Literature and Criticism
Ecocriticism
Postcolonialism Now
Marxist Literary and Cultural Theory

Postsecular Theory
Nations and Nationalisms
Periyar
Popular Culture
Queer Studies
Frantz Fanon
Mikhail Bakhtin
Edward Said
Subaltern Studies
Life Writing

LITERARY/CULTURAL THEORY

DECONSTRUCTION AND POSTSTRUCTURALISM

BIBHASH CHOUDHURY
Gauhati University

Orient BlackSwan

All rights reserved. No part of this book may be modified, reproduced or utilised in any form, or by any means, electronic or mechanical, including photocopying, recording or by any information storage and retrieval system, in any form of binding or cover other than in which it is published, without permission in writing from the publisher.

DECONSTRUCTION AND POSTSTRUCTURALISM

ORIENT BLACKSWAN PRIVATE LIMITED

Registered Office
3-6-752 Himayatnagar, Hyderabad 500 029, Telangana, India
Email: centraloffice@orientblackswan.com

Other Offices
Bengaluru, Chennai, Guwahati, Hyderabad, Kolkata, Mumbai, New Delhi, Noida, Patna, Visakhapatnam

© Orient Blackswan Private Limited 2023
First published 2023

037705

ISBN 978 93 5442 364 2

Typeset in Aldine 401 BT 10.5/13 *by*
Akhil Offset Printers
Hyderabad 500 020

Printed at
B B Press, Noida 201301

Published by
Orient Blackswan Private Limited
3-6-752, Himayatnagar,
Hyderabad 500 029, Telangana, India
Email: info@orientblackswan.com

Contents

Preface	*vii*
Acknowledgements	*x*
1. Introducing Deconstruction *The Term and Its Operative Dimensions*	1
2. Deconstruction *The Terms of Engagement*	18
3. Looking at Texts *Deconstruction and Reading of Literature*	33
4. Structure and After *The Advent of Poststructuralism*	49
5. The Challenge to 'Truth' and 'Reality'	74
6. Poststructuralism Across Disciplines	91
Glossary of Select Terms	108
Suggested Reading	112

Preface

Deconstruction as a term emerged in twentieth-century critical theory primarily through the writings of Jacques Derrida across a series of texts, where he referred to it either by example or by drawing out the processes that enable us to see it at work in culture, literature and other discourses. It is commonplace to situate the emergence of deconstruction in the context of some of Derrida's early writings where we see its engagement across genres, genres; which he continued to focus on in his prolific writing career. In texts dealing with seemingly disparate subjects such as mourning and travel, or translation and law, Derrida worked on the relevance of play in textuality, which is an important aspect of deconstruction.

Usually in approaching a subject one starts with the process of definition. Definition is a framing procedure through which the subject or concept is placed and evaluated. Deconstruction, however, is not something which submits itself to definition in a completely closed sense. Derrida argues that 'definition' is limiting in nature as it involves closure. That is why in approaching the question 'What is deconstruction?', Derrida refrains from giving an answer that would tie it up in a neat package, as it would entail a form of reduction. This is because deconstruction seeks to demonstrate how meaning is provisional and relative to how one assesses a text. In an interview on the subject, Derrida observed that there is 'no "applied" deconstruction' (Brannigan, et al. 217) because it is not something that can be deciphered by means of any formula. He states that it refers to subjects or concepts whose aporia opens up the many dimensions relating to it. 'Aporia' is a Greek word which refers to an experience of irreducibility as it cannot be subsumed by mere opposites within a concept or a text (*Aporias* 14). When we consider a subject or a concept, Derrida argues, there is a tendency to look for meaning, which is a form of 'totalization'. In Derrida's view, this process of totalisation closes off other possibilities that the text itself can facilitate. In other words, deconstruction refers to the recognition of a text's generative ability to go beyond its immediate and apparent structure.

In order to look at deconstruction as a conceptual development in critical theory, it is important to see it also as a response to the tradition of knowledge-production in the West. The tendency to look for meaning in texts or concepts has a very long intellectual history. In his writings, Derrida looks at the ways in which structured knowledge has been privileged in different philosophical exercises. Deconstruction looks at this structuralist engagement with knowledge and responds to it by introducing concepts such as aporia which highlight the playful nature of the text. This book examines the circumstances under which deconstruction has come to occupy its place of importance in critical theory. Along with developments that concern the response to structuralism – seen under the broader rubric of poststructuralism – associated dimensions of critical practice are also looked into in the course of this study.

The question of how deconstruction comes about is not centred around a single site of engagement. In fact, it is the eschewal of any centralising principle that deconstruction draws our attention to. This is done through a process of discursive engagement where textuality is examined and how the process of dismantlement, which is already in place in any given structure, emerges from within the text itself. The structure, then, is one of the 'essentials' that Derrida takes on for the purposes of critique, because he argues that the process of signification that makes up the structure is not absolute, but is the source of play. Spread across a wide array of texts, Derrida's argumentative placement of this aspect of play addresses different textual circumstances which are fraught with internal fault lines. Deconstruction, as Derrida has argued in his various writings, is not a method or an applicable format per se. It is not locatable by itself but becomes evident when a text's interior space begins to militate against its own situation, thereby making the structure unsustainable in an absolutist sense.

In the 1960s, thinkers such as Roland Barthes and Michel Foucault critically responded to the idea of 'structure' by examining the limits of closure with reference to the knowledge question. Foucault discussed the role played by discourse and Barthes considered how the authorial voice was being overwhelmed in the exercise of reading. Although these thinkers have considered different dimensions of the knowledge question, the common thread that connects them with Derrida is the focus on the limitations of the structuralist process. Poststructuralism is often used as an umbrella-term to refer to the critical questioning of structuralist tendencies in twentieth century thought. Deconstruction and poststructuralism are often interlaced and interactive in terms of how the critique of structure is engaged with by both, and there are occasions when overlapping of ideas is common in such movements that bear such labels. This book aims to provide a brief outline of some of these developments with the objective of marking the characteristic aspects of deconstruction and poststructuralism.

While both these 'terms' have occupied space in glossaries, a more interactive examination would facilitate a rewarding dialogue between the reader and the processes that deconstruction and poststructuralism are framed by. No single reading of such complex and dynamic critical processes can aspire to cover the ground that these terms have come to hover over, and this book is no exception. What this book hopes to achieve is to provide a fair idea of what deconstruction and poststructuralism have come to be associated with from the time they emerged in critical space in the middle of the twentieth century. The analysis of these terms, therefore, is keyed with the purpose of introducing and familiarising readers with developments in these fields by means of placing them in an open trajectory so as to see their conversation with the world, and the textual sites they look at critically.

Bibhash Choudhury

Acknowledgements

Writing on deconstruction and poststructuralism is an invite that carries its inevitable questions, and not all are set down neatly on the table to see and run through. My interest in philosophy was first generated by my late uncle Animesh Medhi, to whom I owe the most, for in moving about the field that formed the site of this book, those long conversations with him lit up spaces when navigation seemed difficult. I am grateful to my teacher Ranjit Kumar Dev Goswami for the excitement he brought to the discussions we had, and especially for the ways in which he marked the space of critical theory in the department. I owe so much to my students, who over the years, have been the source of joy and true fillip in reading literary criticism in the classroom. Sreenath Sreedharan has been the one egging me on and his unwavering trust in the project kept it moving, for which I do not have words enough to thank him. I wish every writer has an editor like Namrata Kartik, so meticulous and so focused; it is her truly engaged reading of the manuscript that has seen the book reach its readers in this form. To both Sreenath and Namrata from Orient BlackSwan, a really big 'thank you'.

Chapter One

Introducing Deconstruction
THE TERM AND ITS OPERATIVE DIMENSIONS

Situating the Term 'Deconstruction'

The term 'deconstruction' owes its origin and place in literary and intellectual discourse to the writings of Jacques Derrida (1930–2004). Over the course of many books, lectures, essays and commentaries, Derrida has articulated the term, exploring and shedding light on its different dimensions. In 'Signature Event Context' from his *Margins of Philosophy*, he presents 'deconstruction' as an unsettling of existing stratagems or 'orders': 'Deconstruction does not consist in passing from one concept to another, but in overturning and displacing a conceptual order, as well as the nonconceptual order with which the conceptual order is articulated' (133). The 'problem' associated with the question of a definition in relation to the term has been put in context by Christopher Norris:

> Any attempt to define "deconstruction" must soon run up against the many and varied obstacles that Derrida has shrewdly placed in its path. To begin with, at least, one can perhaps best proceed by way of a series of negative descriptions. Deconstruction is *not*, he insists, either a "method", a "technique" or a species of "critique". Nor does it have anything to do with "textual interpretation", of any kind developed to a high pitch of subtlety by literary critics from Coleridge to Eliot and beyond. (18)

It is evident that deconstruction is not a form of interpretation and it does not offer to *read* and explain textual properties in the conventional way. What, then, does deconstruction entail? In order to respond to such a question, we will have to look at the critical processes employed in approaching the question of 'knowledge' in the modern world. What Derrida suggests is not confined to an interrogation of the modern world or its apparatuses of thought; he examines the very process that goes into the making of ideas which are taken for granted in any given discourse.

This examination involves the scrutiny of the structures through which 'knowledge' is not only articulated, but circulates and participates in society as well. Structures may provide the impression that they are complete and inclusive, and can even be functionally very effective. However, we see how the fault lines in these structures open up once they are closely examined.

Deconstruction involves the interrogation of assumptions set in inherent patterns that go against each other. For instance, we could take terms such as 'reality', 'identity', or 'truth' and locate the way they are seen and accessed through the presence of a foundational logic in their operative process: one of the commonplaces that a lay person would rely on would be that 'truth is truth'. The same logic would apply in the case of a term like 'reality'. Classical philosophical discourses explore such issues by placing what seems to be the most viable framework in that moment in opposition with a competing idea. For instance, a philosophical argument dealing with reality would suggest that one must vouch for only a particular framework of reality and not any other; the debate would concern not what actually constituted the idea of reality but which argument best approximated it. In effect, the history of philosophy is replete with contesting ideas and notions which are set against one another – the contestation being the arguments and critical positions, but not the subject's absoluteness as such. In discussing the validity of these unquestioned notions, Derrida asks us to take another look at the ways in which they have come to occupy our understanding of knowledge. One of the working brackets that Derrida has suggested, in which one could place absolutes such as truth, reality, identity – to name a few – is the 'transcendental signified'.

In placing the practice of deconstruction in context, Derrida examines the function and composition of structure as envisaged by the Swiss linguist Ferdinand de Saussure. Saussure proposed that our understanding of what we make sense of comes from the relationship between the signifier and the signified. The sign, which is the composite of the signifier–signified relationship, is crucial to the way meaning is made and how knowledge is transmitted in culture. According to the structuralist view of knowledge, the meaning-making process rests upon the coherence of the sign. The signifier–signified relationship is projected as the normative engagement in the making of knowledge – that is, what is stated leads to its referred-to object (signified) only, and thus meaning is made. Without the signifier reaching the signified, how would meaning be made? This is the crux of the Saussurean position with regard to knowledge and meaning, a process that is seen as being valid since it is 'structured' and is the source of how we make sense of or articulate a subject.

But is the structure the complete source of what we think of as knowledge? The answer to this question, Derrida argues, remains in abeyance because of the presence of 'play' inside the fabric of the structure.[1] The essay 'Structure, Sign, and Play in the Discourse of the Human Sciences' offers his perspective on certain essentials that have held sway in the 'making' of knowledge.

READING DERRIDA'S 'STRUCTURE, SIGN, AND PLAY'

Presented as a seminar paper in 1966 at Johns Hopkins University, where structuralist imperatives were examined by different thinkers, Derrida's argument demonstrates the problem of assumptions that have consolidated over time through encrustation and acceptance. He points out that a 'rupture' had taken place from the time of thinkers such as Nietzsche, Freud and Heidegger as their interventions challenged and opened upconventional thought-frames to scrutiny. At the beginning of the paper, Derrida brings in the subject of 'structure' and the way it has operated in the understanding of knowledge and meaning. In different ways or manifestations, and even in modes that are not recognised as being part of the process, he argues that structure has been consistently present, so much so that what is actually a provision has acquired the force of foundational reality or truth. In this context, we may look at structures as being operations which facilitate meaning-making processes. When a structure, which operationally is a provision for the 'knowledge' it frames, acquires validity through usage and acceptance, it consolidates into a form of reality or truth. What Derrida implies here is that the functionality of structures comes to be taken for granted because practice does not invite questions about structurality. Consistent presence and practice thus serves to render what is *structured* to be seen as a form of validation.

Without structure, thought is not processed, and within the structure there is the 'centre' which holds the sign in place. The structure is thus taken not just as an inevitability but also as a necessity, for in its coherence lies the crucial implications of meaning. The role played by structure in the production of knowledge is not something that Derrida argues against literally. Nor does he argue for an overthrow of its formation, but what he points out is that structure by its very design bears the condition of 'play', and it is this spin which shows that structures carry their own genesis of unsettlement.

In the opening stage of his paper, Derrida elaborates this point when he points out that 'structurality' has consistently determined the way signs operate. In this context he refers to the tendency of giving importance to the centre or origin. Yet such focus upon the centre has diverted the attention from play which is facilitated by the structure itself. He argues that it is 'unthinkable' that there may not be a centre within a structure. In other words, intellectual history depends on the centre as an essential condition in the formatting of concepts and ideas. He argues that this is a double-bind: on the one hand, structures have centres which govern their structurality, and on the other, the centre is not absolute because play governs it consistently. He elaborates this point thus:

> . . . structure—or rather the structurality of structure—although it has always been at work, has always been neutralized or reduced, and this by a process of giving it a centre or of referring it to a point of presence, a fixed origin. The function of this centre was not only to orient, balance, and organize the structure—one cannot in fact conceive of an

unorganized structure—but above all to make sure that the organizing principle of the structure would limit what we might call the play of the structure. By orienting and organizing the coherence of the system, the centre of a structure permits the play of its elements inside the total form. (*Writing and Difference* 351–52)

Derrida shows how the basis of the meaning-making process is a provisional exercise. It is a question, not of what the structure entails or 'means', but one which points out the problem of absoluteness associated with the knowledge gained from a given structure. Derrida's reading of structure, therefore, draws our attention to the question of play being inherent in the centre of any signification process. This is indeed a radical proposition. Derrida is not arguing that there is something called a centreless condition. He is making a very crucial intervention which is not only radical in what it is proposing, but also undercuts the edifice that relies so heavily on the instrumentality of the centre. To draw on Yeats's phrase, if the 'centre cannot hold', there is only one feasible outcome: collapse.

Derrida invites us to look at the centre for what it entails and how it is programmed to operate in culture. The centre has been taken to have the property of uniqueness because it is the centre which governs the operability of the structure and defines it. Two things emerge in the course of his argument in 'Structure, Sign, and Play in the Discourse of the Human Sciences': first, the centre is understood to be outside the condition of change, and though it is within the structure it is outside because it is not subject to the condition of structurality; second, the centre is seen to possess the attribute of certainty because while play can take place within the structure, it does not dilute the centrality of the centre. In a crucial passage in the essay, he writes,

> The centre is at the centre of the totality, and yet, since the centre does not belong to the totality (is not part of the totality), the totality has its centre elsewhere. The centre is not the centre. . . . The concept of centred structure is in fact the concept of a play based on a fundamental ground, a play constituted on the basis of a fundamental immobility and a reassuring certitude, which itself is beyond the reach of play. (*Writing and Difference* 352)

Many of the terms used by Derrida here acquire significance in the context of his debate with structure: 'centre', 'play', 'totality', 'ground', 'immobility' and 'certitude'. A little further ahead in the essay, Derrida talks about the totalising tendency that has come to be consolidated in culture. This totalisation leads to a grounded assumption (that is, not taken as assumption but as reality) that does not require any scrutiny.

The knowledge-making process conventionally involves totalisation. This is possible when the centre's immobility and fixity is benchmarked as an essential circumstance governing the structurality of structure. In examining this mode of thought-development in Western intellectual history, Derrida argues that the fault lines within the structure do not facilitate the direct signifier–signified equation in the way it is taken to be, that is, the relationship between the two cannot be taken for granted as being fixed or totalised. In the course of the essay, Derrida also examines the limitations of the Saussurean perspective regarding the sign – which is also taken up in *Of Grammatology* – and the notion of 'closure' that comes into the understanding of the relation between the signifier and the signified.[2]

In order to demonstrate how the sense of closure informs structurality, Derrida goes on to examine some of Claude Levi-Strauss's propositions. For instance, Derrida analyses the concept of incest and its configuration in human societies. Levi-Strauss's position in the examination of incest is that of a structural anthropologist, a position from which he looks at the function of the concept and evaluates it. Derrida points out that the accommodation of 'universal' and 'cultural' within the same bracket introduces the problem of categorical logic, as what is all-pervasive cannot be specific to culture. What Derrida invites us to look at is not confined to a predetermined field, which is why he draws upon the argument of Levi-Strauss to substantiate his questioning of the 'structuralist' mode of analysis. In placing the issue of incest as a human practice which is prohibited through adopted moral codes in societies, Levi-Strauss sought to emphasise the validity of the prohibition by showing how the perceived ubiquity of the prohibition could constitute a logic in itself. In this essay, Derrida

Introducing Deconstruction   7

takes up this method of structuralist analysis to demonstrate how it is human agency which grants the condition of 'universality' rather than prohibition being a naturally occurring process. In effect, the condition of naturalness is acquired and hence, man-made.

Though the condition of universality is inextricably associated with how incest is perceived and seen in societies, this is not as natural as something that is derived from nature. The intermingling of natural/universal/cultural dilutes the fixities of these terms so that we have different dimensions of the universal and the natural. It depends on the context in which they are used. The problem, however, is related to the question of deciphering how the signifier for 'natural', for instance, would work? When we have the signifier 'natural', it should lead to that signified which settles it and that signification should be complete, according to Saussure. Yet, that does not happen here. As Derrida points out, the use of 'natural' as a signifier remains constant but can lead to a different signified – a possibility which tears apart the very notion of a transcendental signified. Derrida points this out when he says: 'The incest prohibition is universal; in this sense one could call it natural. But it is also a prohibition, a system of norms and interdicts; in this sense one could call it cultural' (*Writing and Difference* 357). A prohibition is a limitation imposed by human design; it is rule-bound and it is made with the objective of preventing violation. What is considered to be natural, on the other hand, is not man-made and is independent of human determination. That is why the binary arrangement between nature and culture places the two in opposition.

Derrida's contention is that the feasibility of the signifier–signified within a given frame is provisional and not absolute. He exposes the limitations of the nature/culture framing process by demonstrating how the two terms interpellate each other. The centre shifts inside the structure leading to play from within. This demonstrative exercise can be taken as an example of deconstruction. Deconstruction does not involve any form of imposition from beyond the structure. It critiques the assumptions that go into the making of a structure by exposing its internal inconsistencies, as Derrida shows while examining the nature/culture dynamic with respect to the incest prohibition. The crucial point is that the critic does not need to do anything specific to draw out an inconsistency or idea that did not previously exist, but to present the problems associated with the constitutive terms of the structure.

In 'Structure, Sign, and Play in the Discourse of the Human Sciences' Derrida also talks about the connected issues of totalisation and supplementarity. He states that the difficulty of seeing totalisation in absolute terms comes from the various possibilities brought about by the effect of play. These potential alterations cannot be exhausted by any discourse which, in turn, opens up the field to questioning and introduces the condition of supplementarity. Explaining this point, he writes: 'One cannot determine the centre and exhaust totalization because the sign which replaces the centre, which supplements it, taking the centre's place in its absence—this sign is added, occurs as a surplus, as a *supplement*' (*Writing and Difference* 365)

The problem described in the quote above arises not because of the exhaustion of totalisation, but because of how play renders the very exercise of control ineffective. The process of fluid movement unsettles totalisation through play and because the supplement is 'taking the centre's place', the structure is never able to retain itself completely. When we look at a structure – any concept that is expected to be complete in itself – we can see that its totality is a misnomer; it is in a state of incompleteness because its centre is liable to shift depending on how the structure is engaged with or where it is placed.

Deconstruction draws attention to this dynamic dimension of the centre within the structure by demonstrating how the inherent potential for contradictions that defy the logic of its coherence is consistently present. The essay is sweeping in terms of how it projects the circumstances that have gone into the privileging of a metaphysics of 'presence' – a convention that appears valid through continuous references to its own solidity. Sets of binaries are often taken to be valid when it comes to arriving at knowledge – a form of the cancellation of one and highlighting of the other – and is a commonplace technique that is often unquestioningly relied upon. While assumptions that validate the function of binaries seem to have naturalised themselves – presence construed to be more privileged than absence – they are not absolute. Placed differently, the very foundation that grants a binary structure its validity, changes. In effect, the centre changes and the feasibility of its structure being resolutely constant is diluted. 'Structure, Sign, and Play in the Discourse of the Human Sciences' opens up a space where the sign's operative field comes under scrutiny and the very logic that grants the structure its firmness is shown to be fraught with the condition of openness. This opening up is not brought about by Derrida or anyone else; it is not an engineered act. Rather, it is a consequence of play within each structure. Any sign governed by its structurality, is conditioned by the element of play which, though not discerned or realised, unsettles the firmness of the structure and shows that closure of its limits in any form would render it ineffective beyond a given frame.

DECONSTRUCTION ACROSS MULTIPLE REGISTERS

Derrida's early contestation of the structurality of the sign saw him take on principles espoused by Ferdinand de Saussure and Claude Levi-Strauss, among others. Following the 1966 seminar in Johns Hopkins University, Derrida went on to look at a wide range of subject areas from ethics to hospitality, where the same evaluative thread was deployed and deconstruction as a process was seen to be part of/relevant to these fields as well. In this context, it would be helpful to examine some of the ways in which Derrida has responded to the question of deconstruction and its influence in different disciplines. In an interview with François Ewald he was asked,

> Q.: Does the term "deconstruction" designate your fundamental project?

> J.D.: I never had a "fundamental project". And "deconstructions", which I prefer to say in the plural, has doubtless never named a project, method, or system. (*Points...: Interviews* 356)

This response is not ironic. Derrida does not claim any 'ownership rights' when it comes to deconstruction or its recognition, nor does he claim that it is to be 'a project, method, or system'. Deconstruction, in effect, is not a critical tool to be deployed for better exegetical results. The term, evidently, does not lend itself to neat, formulaic encapsulation, and because it resists any structuralist certainty per se, critics have been hard put to 'define it'. Derrida's engagements regarding 'deconstruction' have steered clear of a closed enumeration of its features and his arguments have mostly been directed towards clearing the air about what deconstruction does not entail or concern itself with.

In his early writings, Derrida talked about textualised structures spread across culture and history. This process was demonstrated to have been inherent in the very making of a 'text', whose closed connotations, therefore, invited resistances from within. For several decades after, 'Structure, Sign, and Play in the Discourse of the Human Sciences' came to be seen as *the* frame of reference for engaging with deconstruction. However, as deconstruction entails the recognition of non-closure as a form of entry, he has refrained from committing to any definitive matrix. In the essay, the focus shifts from the sense of closure or totalisation to the acknowledgement of possibilities that challenge the culmination of understanding in a given 'structure'. When he argues that the shifting of the centre within a structure is conditioned by play, he recognises how 'closure' would serve as a form of arresting 'meaning'. This is why Derrida does not commit to any definitive position regarding what constitutes deconstruction. 'Non-closure' thereby comes to serve as a rider for blanketed patterns which definitions are conventionally driven by. As he makes clear in the response to the question of whether deconstruction is a system, method or project, it cannot be construed as such because any conditioning of the process would challenge the very nature of what constitutes a 'text'. Derrida's response to the question about deconstruction being a technique – which is one of the perceptions held with regard to its functionality – places his perspective in context. In the same interview cited above, Derrida responded thus:

> Q.: Could one say that deconstruction is the technique you use for reading and writing?

J.D.: I would say instead that this is one of its forms or manifestations. This form remains necessarily limited, determined by a set of open contextual traits (the language, the history, the European scene in which I am writing or in which I am inscribed with all manner of more or less aleatory givens that have to do with my own little history and so forth). But as I was saying, there is deconstruction, there are deconstructions everywhere. What takes the form of techniques, rules, procedures, in France or in the West, in philosophical, juridico-political, esthetic, and other kinds of research, is a very limited configuration, it is carried – and thus exceeded – by much broader, more obscure and powerful processes, between the earth and the world. (*Points...: Interviews* 357)

How far is location, for example, relevant to the approaches we may have with regard to deconstruction? In his response, Derrida expands his own situation from France to Europe, and then the world, suggesting that the pervasive impact of deconstruction is evident in an awareness of its expanse which cannot be seen only through specificities. Derrida recognises the contextualisation of deconstruction. Equally significant is the awareness that while such determination of limits exists, by its very nature deconstruction extends to situations beyond either France or Europe to a wide variety of locations and conditions. Derrida has himself looked at it in a remarkably extensive range of texts and ideas from Edgar Allan Poe to Paul Celan, from travel to the American constitution, to name just a few. If deconstruction is construed as a process which brings to our notice the fault lines that inhere in a text, does such a process involve a recognition of location? Such questions are pertinent insofar as they enable us to look at deconstruction closely and to examine its engagement in a variety of situations and textual conditions.

The Derridean exercise is not confined to a singular frame of reference, and the deployment of this process has enabled matters of locational difference to find the scope to engage with questions that might have otherwise gone unattended. As Derrida points out in his exposition, the feasibility of deconstruction's processing potential to address situations beyond European or Western contexts alerts us to the wider space that it could have influence over in diverse ways. Derrida seeks to bring to our attention the challenge that lies within any matrix that is structured to project a form of essentialism. As he argues in 'Structure, Sign, and Play in the Discourse of the Human Sciences', deconstruction places the matter of resistance to totalisation not as an imposition to be imported to serve any specific agenda, but as an exercise directed towards bringing to light the limitations that constitute a centralised position, especially when it comes to deciphering 'meaning'. Deconstruction, argues Derrida in this response, is not an absolutely unattached condition affecting our understanding of questions of knowledge. At the same time, Derrida points out that deconstruction is not a 'topical' or context-specific exercise; it is a process whose markings find operative agency outside of the matrices he enumerates in his response.

There are many who have criticised his methodology and process of explication. Barry Smith's letter in *The Times*, dated 9 May 1992, argued against the award of an honorary degree to Derrida by the University of Cambridge, alleging that 'his works employ a written style that defies comprehension' (*Points...: Interviews* 420). Such estimations can be seen not only as a misreading of deconstruction, but also as a refusal to see beyond settled conventions when it comes to the processing of knowledge. Arguments like this frame the resistance to non-closed structures; a resistance that accompanies the comfort derived from the experience of 'closure', of seeing thought and its articulation as providing evidence of the systematised orchestration/organisation of meaning. Deconstruction's impact is thus felt not only in an intellectually closed or determined space/location, but also in asking us to revisit the terms through which questions of knowledge production have been conventionally seen and processed.

How are questions to be asked or framed? This is crucial to how we look at what comes under the rubric of knowledge and meaning. In 'The Deconstruction of Actuality', Derrida points out that the 'question' is one of the keys interrogations through which the approach to knowledge can happen. He points out that writers such as Victor Hugo or Jean-Paul Sartre did not interrogate the manner of critical engagement. To put it another way, in Derrida's view, the apparatus through which one looked at concepts in philosophy was not questioned. The arrival at the functionality of 'meaning' or the purposefulness of enquiry was primarily focussed on the goal of the enquirer. As such, the various processes that impinge upon how we read or approach a situation did not occupy the act of enquiry. The slippages that contest the very nature of argumentation – including the structurality of structure, which Derrida draws attention to in the course of his writings – did not find much space in critical discussion. Derrida argues that when we consider the issue of actuality, what goes into its making and how it is received considerably depends on the dynamics involved in its representation. The enquiry into such dynamics cannot be subsumed through a set of pre-configured conditionals that take the idea of 'actuality' as an idea whose centre would be operative in the same way for all forms of questioning.

Derrida places the nature of intellectual preoccupation pertaining to questioning as a contextual process when he points out that any enquiry regarding what constitutes 'enquiry' was not part of the conventions of the framing of a query. Once a frame is accepted, then there may be intense debate about what is to be done within that bracket, but the frame as such remains uninterrogated. This first premise thus acquires the validity of a foundation and is relied upon in the course of subsequent discourses. He argues that such a foundational premise does not acquire non-violability however sustained its logic is, for any framing process is subject to the circumscribing conditions of its provisionality. In effect, the history of enquiry has often been concentrated in the settling of the debate around concepts, notions, or issues. What is even more crucial, how is a question taken to be a question and what it entails even before a debate can take place within it, is not really looked at as a matter to be pursued. With accretion – which Derrida calls 'sedimentation', that is, the piling-up process through which meanings come to be embedded into certain usages through time and space – there is a layering process that takes over, and it is to this that intellectual attention is primarily given. In the marginalisation of the thought-apparatus as *apparatus*, the focus shifts to the content whereby the tradition of argumentation evolves within a discipline. He refers to Hugo and Sartre as being emblematic of sedimentation.

The discussion on deconstruction thus far has brought to the foreground the resistance to the notion of closure. Any form of bound engagement cannot proceed beyond a point because it is pulled into the central logic that binds it. Deconstruction is not about textuality alone. Over the course of his writings Derrida has taken up concepts, including those that would seem threatened if diluted, in order to demonstrate how deconstruction is at work. One such example is that of law. One of the conditions most associated with law is infallibility. Any idea of law that is subject to alteration or modification will render it void and ineffective. How, then, would deconstruction be seen to be at work when it comes to law and justice? In his essay 'Force of Law', Derrida writes:

> Deconstruction is justice.
>
> Whence these three propositions:
>
> 1. The deconstructibility of law (for example) makes deconstruction possible.
> 2. The undeconstructibility of justice also makes deconstruction possible, indeed is inseparable from it.
> 3. Consequence: Deconstruction takes place in the interval that separates the undeconstructibility of justice from the deconstructibility of law. Deconstruction is possible as an experience of the impossible, there where, even if it does not exist, even if it is not *present*, not yet or never, there is justice. (*Acts of Religion* 243)

The distinction between law and justice is crucial. Justice is not unconnected to law, and the latter exists to ensure fairness. What Derrida locates in the relationship between the two is interestingly placed. Law is subject to what he calls deconstructibility – the condition that it shifts, is mobile and playful – which is why the objective fixity of law may not be able to achieve the goal of justice. Justice and law are interconnected in such a way that both inform one another and in the interval that makes them two different wholes, deconstruction takes place. For justice to be done or to be acknowledged as having been done, the same law can have different consequences depending on how 'what is just' is located in a given case. The fact that law is not fixed and final in all issues that pertain to the administration of justice enables it. If, Derrida argues, both law and justice were governed by unalterable fixity, that would lead to chaos. He writes,

> Law is not justice. Law is the element of calculation, and it is just that there be law, but justice is incalculable, it demands that one calculate with the incalculable, and aporetic experiences are the experiences, as improbable as they are necessary, of justice, that is to say of moments in which the *decision* between just and unjust is never insured by a rule. (*Acts of Religion* 244)

The point Derrida makes here is important and sheds light on how justice *is* deconstruction. Let us take the following situation: a man goes to seek justice saying that this is what the law says and therefore he ought to get it. If justice were to be merely that which the law mandates, then things would get out of hand. As we shall see in Kafka's 'Before the Law' (discussed as a case study in another chapter), adherence to law does not necessarily ensure the administration of justice. A rule or a law is deconstructible, and it is this flexibility which ensures that from the same law, justice may be administered as required. The law's being subject to deconstruction – the sign being governed by play – ensures that justice remains just and fair.

Derrida's wide oeuvre branches out to consider many subjects through which he exemplifies the operative dimensions of deconstruction. Another area which he considers as a site for the demonstration of deconstruction is hospitality. The idea of giving space to the other – as the host does when a guest is accommodated – involves the recalibration of the very structure of space, its configuration altered every time such an interface takes place. In conceptual terms, hospitality marks the sheltering of another concept which is inter-penetrative by nature. The space for the other in the form of accommodation brings about a reconfiguration of the concept itself. Hospitality is thus a process which incapacitates the concept's state of completeness by making space for the other. The host houses the other: this is the proposition forwarded by Derrida with respect to hospitality. Compact and self-containing though it may seem, the very experience of hosting involves providing accommodation to the other, and the other brings about the condition of play through which the concept is resisted from within.

In other words, deconstruction can be viewed as the hosting of that which challenges the host itself. Elaborating further, he says, 'Hospitality is the deconstruction of the at-home; deconstruction is hospitality to the other' (*Acts of Religion* 380). To be hospitable is to invite the other to the space within, and though the other can merge with the host and the two can seemingly become one, by its very condition of otherness it resists the host from the space it occupies. Hospitality thus epitomises deconstruction since it facilitates the housing of the resisting other. From this, many of deconstruction's operative characteristics emerge, including play. The point Derrida emphasises with reference to deconstruction is that a concept's destabilisation is not imposed from outside the host's space but resides within.

The difficulty of approaching deconstruction as a term and what it entails lies within the term's functionality. The concepts that Derrida refers to and draws out for the purposes of exemplification – such as justice or hospitality – can be seen as registers that mark the dimensions of deconstruction. It does not imply that deconstruction has to be approached through the registers Derrida draws upon. Rather, it is the very process of inherent play and resistance to closure which facilitates agency.

NOTES

1. Structuralism and the manner of its working along with the interrogation that emerged in its wake is discussed in the chapters that deal with poststructuralism.

2. Saussure's position regarding the sign and the implications of structuralism in the approach to the question of meaning are discussed elaborately in the section on poststructuralism in this book.

REFERENCES

Derrida, Jacques. *Acts of Religion*, edited by Gil Anidjar, Routledge, 2002.
---. *Basic Writings*, edited by Barry Stocker, Routledge, 2007.
---. *Points...: Interviews, 1974–1994*. Translated by Peggy Kamuf, edited by Elizabeth Weber, Stanford UP, 1995.
---. *Writing and Difference*. Translated and edited by Alan Bass, Routledge, 2001.
Norris, Christopher. *Derrida*. Harvard UP, 1987.

Chapter Two

Deconstruction
THE TERMS OF ENGAGEMENT

KEY REGISTERS AND TERMS OF ENGAGEMENT

Although 'deconstruction' is one word, it incorporates and involves quite a few registers that are connected to its agency. The examination of deconstruction and what it entails would be conducive if these registers are also taken note of, whereby the linkage and engagement between them are looked at effectively. These terms and registers are spread across Derrida's oeuvre and they provide us points of reference through which deconstruction and its processes of critical operations can be accessed. The following registers are not a comprehensive list, but suggest ways of interacting with modes of engagement in order to approach deconstruction as envisaged by Derrida.

Aporia

Aporia is a term whose Greek origins suggest a sense of shift within a thought-frame resulting in irresolution. Its initial placement as a figure of speech was seen as a site that sought to present debaters with the objective of deliberating on how to resolve that which eluded fixity. Appropriated into the scheme of locating the condition of play, aporia is seen as one of the terms through which deconstruction's functioning can be approached. To show how this is processed, Christopher Norris writes, 'deconstruction is the vigilant seeking-out of those 'aporias', blindspots or moments of self-contradiction where a text involuntarily betrays the tension between rhetoric and logic, between what it manifestly *means to say* and what it is nonetheless *constrained to mean*' (19). This tug and pull between what a text is seen to suggest and what challenges that suggestion is inherent in this itself.

It is noteworthy that aporia is not about the possibility of different interpretations of a textual condition. The undermining of what the text appears to project as its meaning is not brought about by something that is injected from the outside, but is an inherent property whose playful ensemble of self-challenging moves make it difficult to settle on a single, unified meaning. The presence of aporia in a text thus opens it up for a reading that is not about contesting interpretations, but the recognition of what becomes evident as indeterminate. Conventionally seen, a term or a concept is understood to be 'clear' in what it suggests or presents as its meaning, and when it is used, that clarity in communication is taken for granted. When aporia is located within a concept, which is inherent and part of the concept itself, the self-regulating principle which makes the structure holding the concept possible faces resistance, which leads to the emergence of contradictions from the inside. This makes it difficult to settle on an absolute meaning with reference to the concept. On the one hand, there is the understanding that an idea or concept will lead to meaning which is clear and identifiable; this is the basis on which knowledge transmission is expected to take place. On the other hand, the blind spots within the idea create conditions of irresolvable uncertainty which make it difficult to subscribe to any one meaning as the only one associated or emanating from that concept or idea. In effect, certain meanings are deferred and remain inaccessible.

This is connected to the notion of time as well. The sense that a concept gives is temporally conditioned, and at any given moment its blind spots lead to inconsequence which is the result of aporia. But aporia as such is not identifiable as this or that because it is the process through which the contradictions within the self-regulated principle of the concept become recognisable. Explaining this dimension of aporia, Richard Beardsworth writes,

> The experience of aporia is one of time and law. The passage of time and the violence of law form two sides of the same coin.

> This experience is "impossible", since experience is predicated upon the present, and since one cannot figure the aporia – that is, bring it into the temporalization of time without losing it – there can be no experience of aporia: or rather, aporia is, in Derrida's terms, an "impossible experience". *One cannot not disavow time.* If time is the delay upon itself, one cannot recognize the delay as such. (101)

Since aporia is not something that is to be seen as having a fixed form, it is not discernible in objective terms. What aporia does is to alert us to the inconsistencies in the self-regulated structure which become evident in such a way that a fixed and confirmed meaning of a concept cannot hold good in an absolute sense. Niall Lucy provides an illustration of aporia which is relevant here.

> The speech–writing opposition, for example, could be said to be sustained by an aporia within the opposition "itself": on the one hand speech can be seen as having to come before writing on the basis only of avoiding that aporia altogether, while on the other the aporia can be shown as necessary to the very constitution of speech and writing as opposites. According to Derrida's deconstruction of the opposition, however, it is writing which comes first. Hence the aporia – or the "aporetic" moment – takes the form of something that cannot be explained within standard rules of logic: writing can be understood as coming after speech only because in fact it comes before speech. In its most general form, this may be put as follows: différance always comes before difference(s). (1)

Deconstruction thus involves the recognition of aporia within a concept, idea or text whose mark is evident when the act of meaning-making is sought to be exercised. This leads to the deferral of the meaning being accessible, and hence whatever is discerned can only be provisionally and contextually relevant. These riders therefore make it imperative to recognise how the activation of aporia within a concept or idea renders the meaning tentative. This is due to what can be called the self-contradiction within the regulated frame of the given concept or idea. Derrida looks at aporia as that condition which does not permit the settlement of meaning, as each text is marked by the aporetic condition.

Différance

Différance is a term coined by Derrida to refer to the conjunction of difference and deferment – attributes which are at work (or rather, play) within a structure, which indicates that a settled, confirmed meaning is not feasible for appropriation from within the frame of reference. Through the term, Derrida points out that instead of the belief that a signifier leads to a signified in an absolute sense, there is a process of deferral – a postponement – and what is taken to be the centre differs because of the condition of play. Christopher Norris elaborates on the process thus:

> In French, the anomalous *a* of *différance* registers only in the written form of the word, since when spoken it cannot be distinguished from the commonplace, received spelling. And this precisely what Derrida intends: that *différance* should function not as a concept, not as a word whose meaning could be finally "booked into the present", but as one set of marks in a signifying chain which exceeds and disturbs the classical economy of language and representation. (15)

Différance resists the centring of identity and is, in effect, the 'absence' of what the sign is believed to be concentrated in, that is, the signifier leading to a settled signified. Différance articulates the absence of a fixed centre and recognises the process of deferral which is not subject to being sensed or known in a manner that closes it down. Différance thus is not a condition of being *present* or being identifiable, but it is an insight into the limitations of the sign which cannot function conclusively. Meaning, then, is continuously in a state of postponement and is different from what the centre appears to project as the settled consequence of the signification process. The centre within the structure is voided by the absence of settled, finalised content, but interestingly there is nothing to occupy that place, for any thing or idea taking that place would render it closed and disengage the structure from being in a state of play. Being in a state of play does not mean that there is some kind of competition for one structure/meaning to take over the position of another. What it implies is that the centre is constantly in a condition of abeyance, and it is this state of the centre remaining unfilled which does not permit any fixity to govern the structure. In effect, différance is that which does not permit totalisation. As Nicholas Royle points out, 'In order to be what it "is", a text is an essentially vitiated, impure, open, haunted thing, consisting of traces and traces of traces: no text is purely present, nor was there some purely present text in the past' (78). The text's consistent slippage into a state where meaning remains out of grasp is a property of the text itself: that there is deferral or postponement is not an initiation from outside the text or an act of indecipherability on the part of the one involved in seeking meaning, but it is the text's pluriform movement within which makes it impossible to settle it down into some kind of centrality. As such, when Derrida draws out the condition of différance as being a constitutive element of textuality, it is not something imposed by any agency beyond the textual site, but an iterated recognition of what is insistently part of a text.

Dissemination

In deconstruction, dissemination is the process of dispersion that breaks out from within the text to thwart any central core from manifesting meaning conclusively. While a text has a structure framing it, the playfulness that makes it a site of dynamic movement does not permit any coalescing, so much so that the exercise of meaning-making has to deal with the process of constant movement which cannot be pinned down. Since there is dispersal, there is no possibility of any settled meaning being accessible at a given time. When the text is seen to *mean* in the course of interpretation, it is a provisional state because the dispersal of the text's energies are never fixed and rooted even if they are taken to be so for the purposes of processing meaning.

> I am reminded of the moment when I first used the word "dissemination" in a certain way – I didn't coin the word "dissemination" – and this was the moment when, writing on Mallarmé, I made much use of the word *pli* . . . *Pli* is a French word with which there is an enormous set of associated words. Of course, you can translate *pli* with "fold", but you can't follow the semantics of "fold" with explication; explication has nothing to do with unfolding; or complication: from

the beginning I was interested in what I call the "originary complication", or contamination, implication, and so on and so forth. (Branningan, et al. 214)

What Derrida calls 'originary complication' here is one of the keys through which we may approach dissemination and its implications for deconstruction. To a question – that which is disseminated – the answer is not to be arrived at by means of locating something within the text. What Derrida suggests is that this process of dispersion is continuous and there is no centre for meaning to be conditioned by in such a manner that the meaning holds good for all time. The provisionality of textual circumstance becomes evident the moment the text is looked at through its signification. As Derrida points out, this does not involve the question of one form of explication rivalling another. It is not about a contest of interpretations; about what a text tries to say or mean. Deconstruction does not eschew interpretation, or is not opinionated as such, but it questions the settlement of any idea as legitimate and valid in a manner that does not recognise the pluriform nature of the textual site. Elaborating this point, Andrew Cutrofello writes,

> There is nothing wrong with interpreting – in fact, we must interpret; all action rests on interpretation – but interpretation must be understood as a risk. To interpret in the absence of legitimation criteria doubtless entails one kind of risk; but to interpret on the basis of an appeal to legitimation criteria – regardless of how they are grounded – is also a risk. In emphasizing the disseminative side of deconstruction, Derrida would in effect be saying, better the vertigo of disseminative politics than the absolutism of dialectical politics. (168)

So what is dispersed is not one interpretation that is hierarchised over others; dissemination is a process of continual movement that refuses the stasis of a centralised position in a text. Dissemination must be seen as part of a textual process in conjunction with other concepts such as différance, undecidability and aporia, each drawing attention to the deconstructive dimension that informs a text and how its agency comes to be manifested through multiple registers.

Grammatology

Grammatology refers to the act and process of writing. In deconstruction and the way in which Derrida locates the term for the purposes of examining its situation in a binary formation where 'speech' is its other, grammatology is seen not in terms of its confinement within a fixed axis but as an iterative condition. Derrida's focus directs us to the limitations of relying on a mode of access which does not permit movement beyond the speech/writing dualism. A restrictive format that is conditioned binarily does not facilitate the ways in which writing (grammatology) is operational outside the stated dualism. Grammatology must be seen outside this binary frame for it to be accessed. Hugh Silverman explains,

> In grammatology, writing has priority – as arché-writing . . . Arché-writing is the textualization of experience, the traces of the letter and the voice which vie for the lead position. But neither written language nor spoken language can succeed, for at their juncture is language itself, cultivated by metaphysics – a metaphysics which calls for its own end. Therefore, to what does language belong? It cannot belong (*ge-hören*) uniquely to the Being of beings any more than it can uniquely hear (*hören*) the call of Being. Language has lost its centre when it incorporates itself into a disseminated self whose meaning is wherever the Logos can be said. But the place in which the Logos is said remains at best a trace (a *grammé*) of a de-logologized language – which we still call metaphysics because it has not quite reached its end, its completion, its fulfilment. (358)

The focus on grammatology, as Silverman points out, does not ensure the hierarchised position of writing, nor does it set writing up against speech by means of cancellation. What it does is to draw attention to the trace that lends itself to the site of the text by situating the unit of writing – a *grammé* which is read as being in a state of dispersal. In *Of Grammatology*, Derrida uses the book to respond to the secondary status accorded to writing by arguing that speech and the understanding that the sign leads to some form of totality are not tenable. He writes, 'The idea of a book is the idea of totality, finite or infinite, of the signifier; this totality of the signifier cannot be a totality, unless a totality constituted by the signified pre-exists it, supervises its inscriptions and its signs, and is independent of its ideality' (*Of Grammatology* 18).

Writing, for Derrida, is crucial as that agency which facilitates the supplement to take over from speech enabling the recognition of the continual dissemination of meaning, thereby resisting any centralisation of meaning. From this perspective, grammatology is seen as liberating and democratic because it does not succumb or submit to any prefigured bracket within which meaning is sought to be confined in an exercise of interpretation.

The bulwark of the Western intellectual tradition rests on the singularity of speech, and its dominance is projected as being that agency which makes it possible for thought to be directly transmitted through a process of signification. He finds this assumption reductive and restrictive as it closes the scope of recognising the validity of play that is part of the constitutive condition of any text. Speech acts are also texts and are subject to the same process through which writing operates, but a traditional privileging of speech has made writing its other, and therefore secondary. In deconstructing this binarily structured privilege, which situates speech in a hierarchised position of supremacy over writing, Derrida opens up the space of the text for re-appraisal.

What this does is to enable him to demonstrate that speech relies on the same registers of operation as writing to appear 'meaningful' for the audience it is directed towards, among which tools of rhetoric and figurative language only end up displaying the condition of play within the sign. In effect, the very understanding that speech is a direct form of communication is underscored by the sign's reliance on the same registers as writing, which is thus a recognition of the destabilisation of the hierarchy of speech over writing.

Logocentrism

Logocentrism is a crucial word in the annals of deconstruction. Derrida draws attention to the insistent concentration of the 'word' (*logos*) in works such as *Of Grammatology* and 'Structure, Sign, and Play' which constitutes the idea of essence in a knowledge system to which the Western intellectual tradition has generally subscribed to. This structural tendency of essentialisation has become so naturalised in the process of addressing questions of knowledge that it is taken for granted as the starting point of critical enquiry. Derrida points out that the reasoning behind the assumption that the word or *logos* is central to the thought-making process is fraught with fault lines that cannot be dispensed with. Does language reflect reality? And if so, is that language and reality an 'absolute'?

Derrida argues that the assumption of the word as having absolute meaning has been consolidated into a form of truth, thereby facilitating the formation of a foundation which has held good over time. Such a foundation works so effectively in the development of discourses, however critically programmed they are, as it suits the movement towards a neatly ordered systematisation of knowledge. What is not recognised in the unquestioning acceptance of the logocentric paradigm, Derrida argues, is that the word is not absolute in terms of what it can deliver when it comes to either truth or reality. Saussurean linguistics seeks to materially legitimise the logocentric argument by drawing on the signifier–signified axis for structure to be the basis of knowledge. Derrida has demonstrated over a series of texts and numerous elaborations, how the understanding that the *logos* is the key to knowledge is unfounded.

The idea that the word, and by extension language, is the primary source of the human approach to reality, has a long history. It goes back to classical debates about the role of language in the discernment of knowledge. These debates orchestrated questions surrounding reality and its nature and how best it could be accessed. The word acquired centrality in these discourses because it was identifiable and tangibly seen as being able to carry out the perceived task of accessing and representing reality. Jussi Backman places this in context when he says,

> The term "logocentrism" was originally coined by the philosopher of life Ludwig Klages to designate the Platonic tendency to subordinate the dynamic unity of life or "soul" to "spirit". For Derrida, it denotes the (no less Platonic) tendency to subordinate the full material reality of discourse and language to λόγος in the sense of an ideal "logical" meaning-structure – and, ultimately, to subordinate all discursive

structures to a "transcendental signified", to λόγος in the sense of an ultimate central "meaning" that would no longer refer to anything other than itself and would thus provide a self-sufficient and permanently accessible centre for discursive chains of references. (69–70)

It is evident that the programming of logocentrism has undergone remarkable consolidation through time and by means of adherence to its tenets; so much so that certain terms have acquired such legitimacy leading to the formation of what is now called the 'transcendental signified'. What logocentrism has done, Derrida argues, is that it has created a sense of security that rests on the efficiency of the word to deliver meaning whenever language is used. This security has enabled the processing of knowledge within a fixed context, and the assumption that this is the mode through which the relationship between the individual and the world can be effectively accessed has held sway in the Western intellectual tradition.

This centrism of the *logos* (word) is inflexible in terms of its operation in language and that is why Derrida's questioning has unsettled an assumption that is perceived to be naturally valid and effective. As Geoffrey Thurley puts it, 'logocentrism: the belief in the power of language adequately to reflect reality. Logocentrism, according to de-constructionist thinking, asserts the empire of truth, a realm of fixed values and positive verities which words successfully evoke and refer to, and novels and poems efficiently mirror' (186).

Derrida's proposition about the centrality of the word, however, has faced questions from contemporary thinkers and philosophers. Is this form of argument one that would enable an adequate response to the question of knowledge? Richard Rorty, for instance, offers a different view. He suggests that one way of examining logocentrism is to situate the idea as a process where the word is privileged but it requires qualification because Derrida's argument seems to propel this *logos* indefinitely. Rorty's contention is that such a placement of logocentrism could cut through the very nature of philosophical enquiry. He writes,

> Derrida's polemic against the notion that speech is prior to writing should be seen as a polemic against what Sartre calls "bad faith" – the attempt to divinize oneself by seeing in advance the terms in which all possible problems are to be set, and the criteria for their resolution. If the "logocentric", Platonic notion of speech as prior to writing were right, there might be a last Word. Derrida's point is that no one can make sense of the notion of a last commentary, a last discussion note, a good piece of writing which is not an occasion for a better piece. (118)

Another aspect of logocentric thought is that it facilitates what Derrida has called the 'metaphysics of presence'. Just as logocentrism is a first principle – that principle which is taken to be the starting point of the thought enterprise – the metaphysics of presence is privileged (and placed in opposition to the idea of absence) and has come to function as the ground for any investigation that aspires to develop cogent discourse. Derrida argues that this tendency is a pre-supposition that is expected to deliver when it comes to knowledge, but in actuality, it does not do so. Terry Eagleton has commented on this aspect of deconstruction when he says that Derrida

> labels as "metaphysical" any such thought-system which depends on an unassailable foundation, a first principle or unimpeachable ground upon which a whole hierarchy of meanings may be constructed. It is not that he believes that we can merely rid ourselves of the urge to forge such first principles, for such an impulse is deeply embedded in our history, and cannot – at least as yet – be eradicated or ignored . . . . But if you examine such first principles closely, you can see that they may always be "deconstructed": they can be shown to be products of a particular system of meaning, rather than what props it up from the outside. First principles of this kind are commonly defined by what they exclude: they are part of the sort of "binary opposition" beloved of structuralism. (114)

As the ground for critical as well as popular discourse, logocentrism and the metaphysics of presence have solidified into strong foundational givens and have served the pursuits of 'truth' and 'reality' quite well. Derrida's questioning of this tendency is a departure from the assumed understanding that truth is accessible and is an identifiable subject that needs to be pursued. In effect, Derrida does not unsettle things by proposing any application of external agency, but rather, he points towards the role played by logocentrist tendencies which have hampered the democratic dimension of Western thought. For Derrida, play is crucial to the understanding of the process through which knowledge comes across, and because of the insistence of play the issues associated with knowledge have to be taken as provisional in terms of what they 'mean'. This is the argument that goes against the foundational practice of logocentrism.

Undecidability

Undecidability is a crucial term in what constitutes deconstruction. When the meaning from a structure or a concept cannot be accessed in a finalised form because the inherent registers lead to multiple possibilities, then it can be said that the condition reflects undecidability. Conceptually, the possibility of arriving at meaning is a sign of closure, for it is that which is done after other possibilities have given way to what emerges as a feasible situation in relation to the concept in question. But this is not so simply organised or structured such that meaning can be directly drawn out and for the equation of concept–knowledge to be closed and thought of as settled. Undecidability is the sign and indication of the structure being open, and not closed. Commenting on the recognition of undecidability being part of the process of locating responsibility, Diane Elam writes,

> [T]he understanding of politics as undecidable is not about refusing to make decisions: it is about refusing to ground decisions in universal laws. We might even go so far as to say that the politics of the undecidable is an insistence that we have to make a decision, each time, in each case – that we cannot avoid making a decision by just applying a pre-existing universal law. (87)

As Elam points out, undecidability is not a form of escape or avoidance; it is deeply embedded in invoking responsibility. It is the disavowal of submission. When the subject is situated and located in a particular matrix, there is the insistence of the apparent textual properties which are immediately evident, and a commonplace rendering would make that appear to be the source of meaning. In surface readings, this possibility is what comes to function as the essence and is taken to *mean* and convey the subject as such. However, as Derrida points out, undecidability is inherent in the text, irrespective of whichever apparent meaning surfaces, for this is not a matter of what appears first. Rather, it is the multiplicity of textual imperatives which insist on being recognised. This plurality deconstructs the idea of a singular thread emanating from the text's centre, leading to undecidability. It ought to be borne in mind that the question of undecidability is not about the interpreter's lack of decision-making but the text's unyielding of a definitive, meaningful circumstance. In other words, the text does not lead to an 'origin' but plays out possibilities that emerge from within.

This tendency of searching for origins is owed to the tradition of looking for a mimetically viable relation between source and meaning that goes back to antiquity. The tracing of what Derrida calls undecidability is from the modern mathematician Kurt Gödel whose use of the term is located as a site for analysis. Elaborating on the genesis of the concept in Derrida, Paul Livingston writes,

> As early as 1970, Derrida suggested an analogy between what he calls the "undecidable" and the incompleteness result discovered by Gödel and first announced in the article "On Formally Undecidable Propositions of *Principia Mathematica* and Related Systems" published in 1931. Derrida draws this connection in the course of a discussion in "The Double Session" in which he juxtaposes an excerpt from Mallarmé's text *Mimique* with a passage from Plato's *Philebus*. The issue raised by both texts is that of *mimesis*, and of the relationship between a representational text, image, or inscription and the "original" that it represents. Mallarmé's text, Derrida argues, makes possible a thinking of *mimesis* whereby it is no longer understandable as the hierarchical relationship between a representation and a (present or deferred) original. Rather, Mallarmé's text gives us to think a "play" of *mimesis* with no original, an order of mirroring defined by *allusion* rather than the hierarchical logic of truth and illusion. (222)

The point that Derrida makes here is crucial for the enumeration of undecidability in the context of deconstruction. Since mimesis is not to be seen as a form of absolute and hierarchically-determined correspondence between text and meaning, the idea that it leads to truth cannot be sustained. What is left is, as Livingston enunciates, is an allusion which extends in multiple directions in the text Derrida draws upon, that of *Mimique* by Mallarmé. In deconstruction, the term undecidability is part of the same axis where other terms such as aporia and play are placed, for each point towards the unsettling of the totalising tendency that deconstruction prises open.

REFERENCES

Backman, Jussi. "Logocentrism and the Gathering Λόγος: Heidegger, Derrida, and the Contextual Centers of Meaning". *Research in Phenomenology*, vol. 42, 2012, pp. 67–91.

Beardsworth, Richard. *Derrida and the Political*. Routledge, 1996.

Brannigan, J., et al. "As if I were Dead: An Interview with Jacques Derrida". *Applying: To Derrida*, Palgrave, 1996, pp. 212–26.

Cutrofello, Andrew. "Derrida's Deconstruction of the Ideal of Legitimation". *Man and World*, vol. 23, no. 2, 1990, pp. 157–73.

Derrida, Jacques. *Of Grammatology*. Translated by Gayatri Chakravorty Spivak, Johns Hopkins UP, 1976.

Eagleton, Terry. *Literary Theory: An Introduction*. 2nd ed., Minnesota UP, 1996.

Elam, Diane. *Feminism and Deconstruction*. Taylor and Francis, 2006.

Froneman, Willemien. "Composing According to Silence: Undecidability in Derrida and Cage's *Roaratorio*". *International Review of the Aesthetics and Sociology of Music*, vol. 41, no. 2, 2010, pp. 293–317.

Livingston, Paul. "Derrida and Formal Logic". *Derrida Today*, vol. 3, no. 2, 2010, pp. 221–39.

Lucy, Niall. *A Derrida Dictionary*. Blackwell, 2004.

Norris, Christopher. *Derrida*. Fontana, 1987.

Rorty, Richard. "Philosophy as a Kind of Writing". *New Literary History*, vol. 39, no. 1, 2008, pp. 101–19.

Royle, Nicholas. *Jacques Derrida*. Routledge, 2003.
Thurley, Geoffrey. *Counter-Modernism in Current Critical Theory*. Palgrave Macmillan, 1983.
Silverman, H.J. "The Limits of Logocentrism (On the Way to Grammatology)". *Man and World*, vol. 17, no. 3-4, 1984, pp. 347–59.

Chapter Three

Looking at Texts
DECONSTRUCTION AND READING OF LITERATURE

READINGS OF TEXTS: DECONSTRUCTION IN PRACTICE

Early in the twentieth century, reading literature was placed within a broader frame that sought to unravel the intricacies of the text through a set of formulaic ordinations, of which New Criticism was the most visibly evident. Although the format proposed by the New Critics took some time to gain currency in academic circles, the process employed involved the taking up of a text which would then be dissected and analysed; its 'meaning' opened up by methodological exegesis resulting in some form of explication which served to situate the analysis for the reader to consider. The texts chosen could range from a poem by John Donne or William Wordsworth to a narrative – the choice determined by the nature of the argumentative tool being employed. This method of 'textual analysis' has come to be the mainstay of criticism for a substantial section of academics and also what Virginia Woolf called, the 'common reader'. The feasibility of reading 'works' in terms of neatly marked sites came under a cloud with the advent of deconstruction, and the notion of textual analysis for the purpose of decipherment of meaning began to be challenged.

It was not a question of one meaning replacing another or a method taking the place instead of an existing one – what was at stake was the overhauling of the critical outlook which opened up grounded frames for scrutiny and examination. Texts which were marked as sites in the politics of meaning-making, found themselves caught up in swings in critical taste which determined how readings are transformed. The same texts became fascinating study-spaces for the exposure of totalising interpretations. The interventions by Derrida have not been part of a jostling game. His method is not one where he partakes in an outsmarting duel; he does not even participate in these critical contests where meaning is the crown to be had. What deconstruction has facilitated is to open up texts beyond the meaning-seeking exercise critics and readers have been engaged in. Deconstruction is not and never has been proposed as some form of replacement in the critical scheme; it is a witness to the cracks that textualisation embeds, and the nature of this witnessing process is not involved in arriving at meaning. What entails the involvement of deconstruction can be evidenced in the examination of how texts bear their own fault lines, of which three examples are given from three different genres: poetry, drama, and fiction.

Case Study 1: Keats's 'Ode on a Grecian Urn'

John Keats's 'Ode on a Grecian Urn' – a poem that drew considerable interest from New Critics, as well as F. R. Leavis – has often been read as a classic which epitomises the play of dualities: transience pitted against permanence. Cleanth Brooks in 'Keats' Sylvan Historian' reads the poem in terms of 'structure' and what its unravelling involves, leading to the decipherment of 'meaning' with the projected view that the historian in the urn transmits its message by the inscriptive meta-phrase: 'beauty is truth, truth beauty'. The same issue has also been explored in a different form by Leavis in a another meaning-marking exercise. Whether it is Brooks's take on the 'well-wrought urn' (the title of the book that carries the essay on this particular ode) or the Leavisite engagement with it, 'close reading' for the purpose of explication appears to be the mainstay of such critical exercises. Brooks and Leavis, insightfully brilliant in their modes of critical engagement, draw out aspects of the poem that may not be discernible to the lay reader. The deployment of their acumen, however, suggests an assurance that the arrival at some form of *telos* with regard to 'meaning' is possible if the tools they employ are pressed into service.

To reiterate, there is no question of privileging one argument over another, one reading placed to displace something else. Critical contestations have been always argumentatively engaged with each other and such processes have only enriched the traditions of reading literature. When we come to the issue of looking at a poem such as 'Ode on a Grecian Urn' and keeping options open in recognising its fault lines that suggest how play conditions its textual circumstance, then possibilities emerge which a meaning-seeking exercise does not quite facilitate. Deconstruction, with respect to a reading of 'Ode on a Grecian Urn' can enable us to situate the text through an examination of the crucial deferment of its perceived essentials, thereby tracing the difficulties of closing it through a narrow matrix that would neatly tie it up for the reader.

Before going into what we can look at through the aegis of deconstruction, it would be relevant to engage with a meaning-pursuing argument, so as to contextualise what Derrida was at pains to draw attention to: namely, that textual understanding cannot simply be reduced to set structures for easy encapsulation. Here is Brooks placing the onus on the reader with the affirmation that Keats expected his poem's meaning to be teased out in the way Brooks has described. Such an orientation situates the poem in a framework where a predetermined set of poetic norms operate, making the exercise in reading a form of conformity with a set formula. It is as if one method of reading is set up against another. Brooks's interpretative proposal thus emerges with considerable forcefulness because he counts on the reader to substantiate his claim. This is a position that does not give the reader much of a choice but to see things in the way that Brooks lays out in the course of his argument:

> It has seemed best to be perfectly frank about procedure: the poem is to be read in order to see whether the last lines of the poem are not, after all, dramatically prepared for. Yet there are some claims to be made upon the reader too . . . He must not be allowed to dismiss the early characterizations of the urn as merely so much vaguely beautiful description. He must not be too much surprised if "mere decoration" turns out to be meaningful symbolism – or if ironies develop where he has been taught to expect only sensuous pictures. Most of all, if

the teasing riddle spoken finally by the urn is not to strike him as a bewildering break in tone, he must not be too much disturbed to have the element of paradox latent in the poem emphasized, even in those parts of the poem which have none of the energetic crackle of wit with which he usually associates paradox. This is surely not too much to ask of the reader – namely, to assume that Keats meant what he said and that he chose his words with care. (Brooks 142)

It is crucial that this placement of reading priorities be seen not merely as an exegetical tool but also as a formula which the reader is expected to subscribe to. The New Critics often projected their mode of analysis as resulting in an interpretation gained through a 'valid' process, at the expense of other such projections.

It is in this context that what we know of as deconstruction is to be located, especially with regards to the question of a text such as 'Ode on a Grecian Urn'. The first thing that needs recognition is that deconstruction does *not* entail a contest of interpretations, for to engage deconstruction in reading this ode of Keats is to steer clear of the meaning-pursuing exercise. Let us look at a few lines from the poem and see how certain critical processes envisaged by Derrida come to have a bearing on the way we look at it textually:

> O Attic shape! Fair attitude! with brede
> Of marble men and maidens overwrought,
> With forest branches and the trodden weed;
> Thou, silent form, dost tease us out of thought
> As doth eternity: Cold Pastoral!
> When old age shall this generation waste,
> Thou shalt remain, in midst of other woe
> Than ours, a friend to man, to whom thou say'st,
> "Beauty is truth, truth beauty," – that is all
> Ye know on earth, and all ye need to know. (Keats, 'Ode on a Grecian Urn')

The 'conclusive' assumption that the speaker sees the urn as asserting through the adage of beauty and truth being interpenetrative – worked out here through a series of placements as time's tested attestation – is, however, not as neatly settled as it is generally taken to be. The idea that the urn 'teases' human 'thought' marks it as active in terms of what it drives home even though it is 'silent' as a form. As can be seen in this stanza, the framing of binaries to situate the circumstance of time's movement on the one hand and the continuity of the urn as a truth-serving object is set upon a very fragile condition: the viability of the urn outlasting generations to persist with the same message. There is thus a taken-for-granted, unquestioning reliance on the urn's ability to 'remain' a 'friend to man', a condition which suggests that this kind of dependence is not founded either on evidence or based on fact. It shows that Keats is referring to a metaphorical extension which pits two dimensions of time against each other: the more visible temporality of generations which are being constantly replaced one after another, against the urn's ageing – it is, after all, the 'child' of 'slow time' and is impacted by this movement, however imperceptible.

What we then see, textually, is that the notions that the urn has *remained* and will *remain* are hypothetical orientations which present modes of regulation – slow time (as applied to the urn) and a faster, more impactful evident passage of time (as applied to people). The play here is much more interesting than what a framing of opposites along the lines of the transience/permanence model would suggest and effectively close off – that dimension is not conclusively determined, but kept open throughout the poem. The possibility of the urn perishing eventually at the hands of 'slow time', though not an immediate contingent reality, is nevertheless a hovering feasibility that undercuts the seeming idea of eternity.

This embedded layering of a gradual sliding of time's slow wheels upon which the notion of perceived permanence is seen, thus has its bearing on the poem's most powerful axiom of truth and beauty being a timeless lesson that humanity ought to learn from the urn. With the urn itself subject to the temporal wheel, albeit slowly, its 'truth' too is not an absolute nor is the notion of beauty. In the Keatsian conceptual universe, beauty has many connotations, among them the drawing in of imagination which serves to envisage an interconnected understanding of the terms 'truth' and 'beauty' with each interpenetrating the other. With truth and beauty taken to be absolute values, imagination's vehicular orientation would suffice to present a compact world view of the settled Keatsian cosmos. Yet, as the poem's self-evident textual markings show, the play is not between time and stasis, but its varying pace; one immediately discernible, the other not quite so. The fragility of 'thou shalt remain' not being immediately evident allows the binary of art/life to come out quite effectively.

It is not just the New Critics who have bought into this meaning-pursuing exercise as a reading necessity. Any argument that seeks to unravel the dynamics of the truth–beauty equation with the aspiration of the critical enterprise being closer to the poem's essence, approaches it through a lens which does not consider that fault lines may be at work insistently, unsettling the very premise sought to be established by the argument. Helen Vendler, for instance, in a brilliant reading of the poem draws out the nuances of the text, its ambiguities, and its playfulness, marking the tension that persisted in Keats's experience – Vendler refers to extra-textual circumstances to argue how Keats was occupied with dilemmas of articulation – but the analysis comes to 'conclude' that the affirmativeness, in spite of its strong argumentative force, cannot quite hold its ground when the temporally shifting urn's slippage opens up in the context of its 'slow' submission to time, thereby arriving at a form of 'closure'. Vendler writes,

> The urn can speak of nothing but itself, and its self-referentiality is nowhere clearer than in the interior completeness of its circular epigram, which encounters our ironic sense of its limitation. When the urn says, commenting on its own motto, that that is all men know on earth and all they need to know, we realize that it makes that announcement from the special perspective of its own being, the timeless being of the artwork in the Platonic realm where Truth and Beauty are indistinguishable. It speaks to us from its own eternity, at once so liberating and so limited. Keats's choice of a circular frieze, rather than a linear one, confirms the urn's self-enclosing and self-completing form. (133)

Vendler also suggests that rather than the urn being a historian (Cleanth Brooks's designation), it is an epigrammatist. A figuration that places an even greater responsibility upon the urn to pronounce tenets for humanity to consider and adhere to. Derrida's interventions regarding positions of reading does not negate the conclusions that either Brooks or Vendler have arrived at. What we can see from the insights of his reading process is that the grounds upon which readings as such are founded are not reflective of absolutes, but are inherently conditioned by the predicament of play. 'Ode on a Grecian Urn' offers us a rich site to look at and engage with, its assured 'values' and accrued imperatives over the last two centuries making critical reading by acknowledging the insights of deconstruction even more rewarding.

Case Study 2: Shakespeare's *Hamlet*

Among the most commented and deliberated upon texts in world literature, Shakespeare's *Hamlet* has been the critic's playground as well as the site which has refused to submit to structured attempts to pin it down. If a text ever became the space of such critical contestation that one needed to break down its textual properties in order to arrive at meaning, then *Hamlet* would surely be at the front of the line. Jacques Derrida has reflected on *Hamlet* in *Spectres of Marx*, the reference informed by his engagement with the ghost, the spectral dimension occupying his argument throughout the book. In one passage on the nature of the ghost's significance in terms of how it is configured and placed within the apparitional logic that binds it to the play, Derrida talks about the signature that embeds the condition of repetition. He writes,

> Repetition *and* first time: this is perhaps the question of the event as question of the ghost. *What* is a ghost? What is the *effectivity* or the *presence* of a spectre, that is, of what seems to remain as ineffective, virtual, insubstantial as a simulacrum? Is there *there*, between the thing itself and its simulacrum, an opposition that holds up? Repetition *and* first time, but also repetition *and* last time, since the singularity of any *first time*, makes of it also a *last time*. Let us call it a *hauntology* . . . And the opposition between "to be" and "not to be"? *Hamlet* already began with the expected return of the dead King. After the end of history, the spirit comes by *coming back* [revenant], it figures both a dead man who comes back and a ghost whose expected return repeats itself, again and again. (*Spectres of Marx* 10)

What Derrida calls a 'hauntology' serves his reading of the conditions of repetition and appearance, facilitating his examination of the *deferral* of the potential each ghost movement bears. The beginning and the end – spots in the temporal calendar – do not terminate or initiate what marks the new in society, for even after the spectre of Claudius's reign is over we see the cyclic gathering of the fallout for the nation; Fortinbras being the supposed ennobler carrying the weight of a past not of his choosing. Hamlet was similar: his situation was not chosen by him. In a much larger movement, Hamlet is caught in a cyclical web where comprehension is out of reach. Derrida points out that it is not about the protagonist's thought-acumen but the very nature of 'knowledge' as such that eludes him, remaining out of his hand. If Hamlet's father by his proverbial *return* realises in visible terms the commandment of inevitability working here through the fabric of 'revenge', it is only as a figure of incompletion that his appearance can acquire validity. The ghost remains a repeat figure, after Hamlet falls at the end of the tragedy. Fortinbras finds his spectre haunting the land he has come to occupy.

Polish poet Zbigniew Herbert captures this hovering spectral phenomenon of Hamlet in his 'Elegy of Fortinbras':

> Adieu prince
> . . .
> I go to my affairs This night is born
> a star named Hamlet We shall never meet
> what I shall leave will not be worth a tragedy
>
> It is not for us to greet each other or bid farewell we live on archipelagos
> and that water these words what can they do what can they do prince
>
> (186–87)

In Fortinbras's 'new' world the old never lets go, its spectral visitation ordained through another matrix, that of the Hamlet figure – a repetition which recycles the pressure of expectation coupled with the necessity of correction. This deferral remains in its state of postponement; the meeting does not take place. 'We shall never meet', says Fortinbras, something similar to Hamlet's inability to have a conversation with his father. The conversations in the play are never complete, the spectre of a promise remaining just that: a promise, unrealised.

Derrida's numerous markers have been variously appropriated – not necessarily ones where deconstruction is his focal subject – with the understanding that the consistency of his critical thread would bear out the argumentative implications of what is his signature mode: the unsettling of closure or totalisation for the recognition of the inherent play in any structure. Shakespeare's *Hamlet*, argues Christopher Prendergast, offers itself as a textual site for the evidencing of différance, a form of deferment that does not enable the consolidation of the play's moral energies within its fold. Given that the play's ethical imperative hinges on the settling of accounts by Hamlet as an exercise in correction, 'justice' becomes crucial both as the ideal and as a trope which the protagonists try to read as their own.

Prendergast does not make a case for one interpretation being more viable than another – the argument is worked through a different matrix, that of the examination of the grounding notions of the play, such as justice and fidelity. Hamlet as an individual is placed within a contested site where he is expected to negotiate his choice. The point is not what he chooses, but crucially, what he sees his choices as. In locating justice, for instance, within his own understanding of its essentials, he is compelled to give it a subjective spin and posits this against what officially holds good for someone like Claudius. The play is not just between rival-defined values – Hamlet versus Claudius – it is the embedding of undecidability as part of his own figuration of justice that makes him dither.

The centre, as Derrida points out in reading the condition of play in any given structure, keeps shifting, keeps moving about in such a way that questions with their insistent baggage – religion or ghosthood for example – infiltrate Hamlet's notion of justice. Hamlet's reading thereby is a constant reassessment of imbibed values which he cannot bring himself to settle upon conclusively. In analysing Hamlet's indecisiveness, the focus is commonly seen to be on his individuality, and in his personhood is located the traces of the proverbial delay. What Derrida's insightful unshackling of the accrued layers that compress totalisation into a conceptual given has done is enable us to also see Hamlet beyond a person-centric idea, a process which is not placed within any interpretative domain.

Concepts such as justice carry a deterministic paradigm which is considered to be essential for its operational purposes. How can justice be thought of as having its bearing if its centre keeps shifting? Constancy and consistency are constitutively structured within the paradigm of justice and therefore, it is seen as being effective. An interesting case in point in Shakespeare's representation of Hamlet is that we get to see his position from a particularity with which he frames justice. He occupies the space of the arbiter; he has to be seen as carrying out justice – but herein lies the catch. He cannot conclusively ascertain whether his understanding and interpretation would be the objectively viewed one as well. He is not merely fighting an interpretational battle, he is befogged by the play that destabilises the centre of his idea of justice. The conceptual solidity of justice faces challenges that he cannot readily negotiate: Hamlet sees Claudius at prayer, a situation he is unable to make sense of adequately as it challenges his idea of just action. Another example which reflects the undecidability paradigm for Hamlet can be seen in the play-staging scene where his search for clues in the king's reaction does not satisfy him enough. Is the justice that he is holding out for one that would suffice for everyone? Totalisation eludes him and he is left wondering what may be the ideal for him – the ideal that he has held onto while embarking upon the enterprise of revenge has not been consistent enough for him to zero in on. Prendergast locates in this tendency a materialised eschewal of closure and argues that,

> Justice and time go together by virtue of the former by reference to a past and a future: on the one hand, an original wrong evoking an historical-causal chain leading back to a primary transgression, and, on the other hand, a final rectification of that wrong, a final solution in which the historical, the political and the ontological will come together in a final moment of pure presence, realized in some for form of material embodiment. This is the conception Derridean deconstruction tirelessly exposes to critique. (46)

The chain of events do not add up to a neat package. The sense of incompletion and deferral that is the play's signature is not simply the plot configuring Hamlet as indecisive – which is another track to be looked at – it is more insistently built into the text's properties, as the examination of repetition and justice demonstrate. Deconstruction is not driven home from some apparatus outside the text of *Hamlet*. The play's numerous registers move through fault lines that cannot seamlessly merge. Chiara Alfano takes up this issue further when the role of the listener is visualised with Derrida being a part of the audience, his ears picking up the ghost's voice and what the entire spectrology entails:

> Yet, when Derrida writes that the apprehension of the ghost is tuned into frequency he is not primarily saying that we must actually listen for the sounds that the ghost makes. What is at stake with frequencies is not only hearing in the common sense, but also the inscription of the spectre's insistences, rhythms, waves, cycles, periods and radical fissuring of Being on the ear. This plurivocal term – *fréquence* – will therefore allow us to prick up our ears to both the ghost's voice in *Hamlet*, as well as to how Derrida listens and responds to the voice of the Thing Shakespeare in *Specters*. (217)

What the Derridean reading process brings to the table is not an interpretational premise aimed at enabling us to make sense of the plot. It is the exposure of the fault lines that unsettle the givens which earmark the tragedy's movement – a process which, it is important to point out, does not seek to invalidate *Hamlet* as a play. Nor do these critiques of conditions such as justice and repetition derail one valuation at the expense of another. Deconstruction here serves to facilitate the critique of the closure in the text by demonstrating how no notion or position is adequately self-sufficient to become *the* key to its interpretations.

Case Study 3: 'Before the Law' by Franz Kafka

Play in fictional narratives opens up when engaged with, one example of which can be seen in the reading of Kafka's very brief story 'Before the Law'. Derrida posits the Kafkesque interrogation of accessibility in the story thus: 'How to gain access to the Law? How can one touch it? What is progress towards the Law?' (*Acts of Religion* 172). This question of access is associated with that of knowledge, not just of the self, but also of the 'system' in which the individual is placed. Access and denial are dominant tropes in Kafka's world view, and the interplay between the state and the individual consistently interrogates the nature of the conversation across his fictional space. Why is it that such knowledge remains incomplete? Putting the self in the formatted space of a system that refuses to yield, however, is not as closed a binary equation as is made out to be.

In the story by Kafka, a man arrives 'before the law' in order to get entry, but he is faced by a doorkeeper who denies him permission. The man is insistent but how much ever he tries, no amount of cajoling or gifting facilitates his entry into the world of law. The doorkeeper's constancy is affected by his unwavering denial to the man who spends months, then years, waiting for his turn. Nothing is altered. What changes is the man's physical state, and with the passage of time he realises that he is gradually decaying and soon will be gone. His eyesight fails him and as he grapples with his final state, he asks a supplementary question, this knowledge now necessary to situate himself and the purpose with which he embarked in this whole enterprise.

> "Everyone strives for the law," says the man; "so how is it that in all these years no one except me has ever asked for admittance?" The doorkeeper perceives that the man has reached his end, and so as to be heard even as the man's hearing is failing, he shouts at him, "No one else could gain admittance here, because this entrance was intended only for you. Now I will go and shut it." (Corngold 69)

The universality ascribed to law is what makes it what it is, for it is not an individual prescriptive apparatus. The ideas of equality and accessibility are embedded within the matrix of what is taken to be legal and the man's arrival at the door is based on that assumption's pervasiveness – like anybody else, he too will have access, for is that not the first condition of law? Yet not only is his attempt thwarted, but he is also prevented from interacting with the law, and his final realisation is that the law for him is individually programmed and conditioned.

What emerges, in Kafka's placement, is the opposite of what is taken for granted: law is neither accessible nor equal. On first reading, the story shows the ironic dimensions of 'law' – the inaccessibility framed within the garb of universality and the ascribed component of equality turning out to be highly individualised. This is evident as the story is read and the satire comes through in Kafka's final thrust where the very edifice of law's normative character collapses.

What is interesting, however, is not just this ironic impingement of the legal condition. The narrative is oriented to present another more telling argument that is part of what is taken as law. Law, as Derrida argues, is not a mere playing out of the imperatives in a just/unjust equation. Its complexity is embedded in a much more insistent inevitability:

> ... by deconstructing the partitions that institute the human subject ... at the measure of the just and the unjust, one does not necessarily lead towards injustice, nor to the effacement of an opposition between the just and unjust but, in the name of a demand more insatiable than justice, leads perhaps to a reinterpretation of the whole apparatus of limits within which a history and a culture have been able to confine their criteriology. (*Acts of Religion* 247)

It is this very process of examination of the limits that circumscribe the Kafkesque drawing of 'law', its irony so crucially embedded in it, which Derrida prises open. As he points out, it is not about one preference over another – the just/unjust equation for instance – but, more significantly, the very notion of law which is opened up in this examination. The man in Kafka's parable can be seen to have been treated unfairly by the law in that he was not even given the scope to interact with it or present himself to it. In effect, the seeming blindness of the law lays bare its inaccessibility which served to deny the man the opportunity of the just audience he craved for. A reading along this line of argument focuses on the subject as victim, a line which we see played out in Kafka's longer fictional works as well, such as *The Trial* and *The Castle*. This view pits the human subject against a remorseless, ungraspable, and therefore, unidentifiable opposition. 'Before the Law' presents a protagonist placed in a similar predicament. His insistence and appeals, even enquiries of a very gentle nature, do not yield anything. The doorkeeper makes it clear to the man that he has considerable authority which he is in a position to exert and exercise. But law is not vested in one face or one step that the man is confronted with; law is a pervasive continuity:

> Since the door to the law stands open, as always, and the doorkeeper steps aside, the man bends down to look through the doorway into the interior. When the doorkeeper notices, he laughs and says, "If you find it so tempting, just try to go in despite my prohibition. But note: I am powerful. And I am only the lowliest doorkeeper. But outside each hall stands a doorkeeper, each more powerful than the last. The mere sight of the third one is more than even I can stand." (Corngold 68)

The man's perception that he is not equipped to overwhelm the doorkeeper and therefore it is conducive to wait, is inbuilt into the parable's mechanics of power. Things remain where they are in terms of the man's interface with law. In effect, he succumbs and disappears and the unrelenting constancy of law as an insurmountable barrier is retained. This dimension of the individual going numb in front of the law determines reading patterns when it comes to the story. Argumentatively, the man fails in his attempt and the law, with its tiered structure, rebuffs the man at the very first hurdle. It, thus, seems to be commonplace to assume that the story is about the victimhood of the man and the stoniness of law, which is represented by the doorkeeper.

Looking at the text beyond this binary, we can locate in its architectonics what Derrida calls criteriology and the fault lines that lie embedded in it. Literary readings and the way they focus on 'themes' and 'techniques' through an isolation of 'characteristics' rely considerably on assumptions to validate the arguments. In this story, the reliance on the individual/law binary opposition is starkly placed to magnify the power of law over the man. The face of law, as he sees and encounters it, is an imposing figure: represented here by the doorkeeper. He is the 'lowliest' in the scale by his own estimate and pronouncement, yet the man sees in him a force that is too strong to be challenged. This configuration of the two positions – of law and the individual – is magnified at both ends. Just as the doorkeeper's confidence and assured control is shown, we see the weakness of the man; his gradual succumbing to decline as he waits marks him as being even weaker than he would have otherwise been seen in any other context. What appears deterministic here is a play of circumstance tailored to emerge as a totalisation of the two counters: individual and the law. Yet, neither is the law as represented here the flagbearer of its essence, nor is the man the epitome of humanity. That the story is read in a manner where the symbolic inference makes this appear as a form of universality is a grounded assumption that is not questioned or examined.

The law, in the story, is governed by the condition of provisionality. In the first place, there is no way of knowing from what we receive textually whether the encounter is with law as an absolute. The doorkeeper's ambiguous station and his operative protocols do not bear out the force of law as it is taken to be. That is why the man is in a conundrum. The law he knows is not what he encounters. This also opens our reading to facilitate the condition of play. The centre of law is a centre that keeps shifting, for the man it is one (the door he arrives at is his alone) and for another man, another. There is no way of determining what constitutes the essence of law, and without that being known how is one to conclude, decisively, that the parable presents the idea of the stoniness of law with regards to the epitome of humanity?

Secondly, the configuration of the doorkeeper is placed in such a way that it is only an indication of the entrance to law, not necessarily the law itself. When the doorkeeper projects his own position as one of power in a hierarchical scale, what is the nature of this hierarchy? A hierarchy of doorkeepers? What is the extent of his knowledge, or his jurisdiction? Is the doorkeeper equipped enough or entitled to such knowledge which would place him in a position from which he can be the arbiter and the face of law even when he is a doorkeeper? These questions remain unresolved, primarily because they are shoved behind the text, not removed, but kept under erasure. These fault lines go into the configuration of law in the story surface when the apparent binary opposition between the man and the doorkeeper is probed closely, exhibiting thereby the play that causes the centre to become fluid.

REFERENCES

Alfano, Chiara. "Strange Frequencies: Reading *Hamlet* with Derrida and Nancy". *Derrida Today*, vol. V, no. 2, 2012, pp. 214–31.

Brooks, Cleanth. *The Well-Wrought Urn,*. Denis Dobson, 1949.

Corngold, Stanley, editor and translator. *Kafka's Selected Stories*. Norton, 2007.

Derrida, Jacques. *Acts of Religion*, edited by Gil Anidjar, Routledge, 2002.

---. *Spectres of Marx*. Translated by Peggy Kamuf, Routledge, 2006.

Herbert, Zbigniew. *The Collected Poems 1956–1998*. Translated by Alissa Valles with Czeslaw Milosz and Peter Dale Scott, Ecco, 2007.

Keats, John. *The Complete Poems*, edited by John Barnard, Penguin, 2007.

Prendergast, Christopher. "Derrida's Hamlet". *SubStance*, vol. 34, no. 1, 2005, pp. 44–47.

Vendler, Helen. *The Odes of John Keats*, Belknap Press, 1983.

Chapter Four

Structure and After
THE ADVENT OF POSTSTRUCTURALISM

A BRIEF ACCOUNT OF STRUCTURALISM

The beginning of the twentieth century saw a shift in the way literary texts came to be read and interpreted. This was brought about by numerous factors, including a questioning of the author-centric reading process which was sought to be replaced by a more concentrated engagement with textuality. The focus on the text and its properties was argued for by T. S. Eliot and the New Critics, for example, in order to draw out nuances that were often sidelined in the approach to literature in the nineteenth century.

Early-twentieth-century critics sought to reorient questions of purpose and intention that had informed the reading of texts (to a considerable degree) in order to examine the intricacies of the text and how it operated to govern 'meaning'. While the Anglo-American critical focus was directed towards textuality and the importance of reading literature without dealing very much with authorship or 'background', there was another paradigm shift taking place in linguistics which was to have a remarkable impact in areas beyond its immediate field of study. It is to the work of Swiss linguist Ferdinand de Saussure that this shift owes much in terms of its genesis and orientation.

Saussure argued that there was a system of signs that operated to construe the meaning-making process through the use of language. He focused on the value of 'structure' as a 'system of signs', the understanding of which is crucial in coming to terms with the emergence of 'meaning' across languages and disciplines. When Saussure's *Course in General Linguistics* was posthumously published in 1915, it inaugurated a new spacing of the field of language study with the sign occupying centre stage. The key term for Saussure was 'sign' and its operative accompaniment was 'structure'.

How is the idea of structure to be assessed and approached? While there are specific features that apply to disciplines spread across the linguistic, literary and cultural spectrum, there is a commonality in the way structure functions. Jean-Michel Rabaté places the matter cogently when he writes, 'The broadest definition is that a structure is an abstract model of organization, including a set of elements and the law of their composition. Even when the nature of these elements varies considerably, what matters is the inner coherence of the whole' (6). The key term here is 'coherence', in that a structure makes sense because it functions as a format that it is held together by a unified principle. For Saussure, this principle is the system of signs. A structure, specifically linguistic structure, is governed by the centrality of the sign and for any meaning to be processed, it is this functionality which must be operational. 'As the name suggests, post-structuralism implies a certain kind of relationship to structuralism, though this begs immediate questions about the nature of the connection. What is meant by structuralism itself? And what kind of relationship exists between structuralism and poststructuralism?' (Howarth 7).

It is noteworthy that Saussure's engagement with the sign as a system was part of a linguistic paradigm through which he sought to highlight the agency that contributed to the meaning-making process in language. Language was seen by Saussure as a structurally constituted design and its importance was expansive enough to accommodate the intricacies of cultural evocation. Since his focus was on the parameters provided by language, the references to 'culture' were oriented to sustain his argument about the sign being central to how it functioned in society. Joshua Katz has argued that Saussure was not perhaps looking at the possibilities or implications of his focus on the sign as the agency that would open up frontiers of understanding well beyond the limits of linguistics: 'A further consequence of the *Cours*, and one that Saussure himself never could have predicted, was the application of structuralism to large texts: poems, stories, novels, not to mention dreams' (Katz 125).

How far is this assumption regarding the Saussurean processing of structuralism as a merely linguistic enterprise to be taken? In a recent study on the impact of *Course of General Linguistics* after more than a century, Beata Stawarska argues that Saussure very much anticipated the developments that came about in the field even though the engagement with the sign was primarily seen as a linguistic act. Stawarska places the relevance of the Saussurean model within a wider ambit that accommodates the sociocultural dimensions of language. Examining the implications of the structuralist process, Stawarska writes, 'language is unique in that it pervades all areas of social life. Members of a society are not necessarily members of educational and/or religious institutions in their life. However, the language institution binds them all insofar as they necessarily communicate with one another. Just as there is no language without society, there is no society without language' (51).

This expansive engagement of the sign in the structuralist paradigm suggests the wide applicability of the analytical process initiated by Saussure at the beginning of the twentieth century. A reading of the advent and subsequent development of structuralism would therefore entail the processing of both the linguistic and cultural parameters it came to be associated with as it was situated through different social registers across a range of disciplines. The placement of this Saussurean understanding, at its most immediate level, would enable the location of its involvement in fields other than linguistics as well. In his *Course in General Linguistics*, Saussure argued that language is a 'system of signs' that operates in society:

> Whereas speech is heterogeneous, language, as defined, is homogeneous. It is a system of signs in which the only essential thing is the union of meanings and sound-images, and in which both parts of the sign are psychological . . . Linguistic signs, though basically psycho-logical, are not abstractions; associations which bear the stamp of collective approval-and which added together constitute language -are realities that have their seat in the brain. Besides, linguistic signs are tangible . . . Language is a system of signs that express ideas, and is

therefore comparable to a system of writing, the alphabet of deaf-mutes, symbolic rites, polite formulas, military signals, etc. But it is the most important of all these systems. (15–16)

This placement of language as 'a system of signs' is crucial in the context of what constituted structuralism. Saussure went on to engage with this signification process by highlighting the manner in which the signifier and the signified function in the making of the system of signs, a design that has overarching bearing on how meaning is processed in language. Seemingly concerned with the meaning-making process in language, Saussure's intervention in the analysis of the sign system inaugurated an important dimension in the field of humanities and cultural studies. By situating the study of and approach to language as a structure, Saussure offered an approach that became an enabling reading strategy across disciplines. Prior to his analysis of language being regarded as *the* modality through which structures could be examined across a variety of fields, different disciplines in the humanities and social sciences operated individually within their specifically oriented limits. The Saussurean offering brought about interesting opportunities to analyse situations in and across culture and literature which were unheralded in these fields and disciplines.

In order to look at structuralism and its emergence in the intellectual and cultural history of the twentieth century, it is imperative that a mapping of its fields of impact be assessed through an appraisal of its characteristics as well as the processes which went into its making. Claude Levi-Strauss, in his path-breaking *Structural Anthropology* for instance, took this structuralist paradigm to read and analyse the formative dimensions of society, looking at the intricacies involved in the ways in which cultural conditions embedded in these formative dimensions operated and functioned. In his chapter titled 'History and Anthropology', Levi-Strauss states, 'In the light of modern phonemics we can appreciate the immense scope of these propositions, which were formulated eight years before the publication of *Cours de linguistique générale* by Ferdinand de Saussure, which marked the advent of structural linguistics. But anthropologists have not yet applied these propositions to their field' (Levi-Strauss 20). Levi-Strauss extended the propositions of structuralism to the study of culture and society, thereby highlighting the effectiveness of the process of structuralism in analysing formations and behavioural patterns, along with customs, traditions and practices.

What he drew attention to was that even though societies were unique in their own way, there were underlying structures that could be discerned by the study of certain systems. This process required an examination of the ways in which structures played their part in the consolidation and identification of distinctive formations within these societies. It was not just society as such, but the intricacies of the minute systemic procedures engaged in the making/producing of units of social structures that Levi-Strauss looked at from the structuralist point of view. *Structural Anthropology* is a path-breaking documentation of social and cultural systems which is multi-pronged in its approach, accommodating as it does questions extending from kinship and family to identity, habits and customs. When Levi-Strauss took the structuralist paradigm beyond the field of linguistics it opened up the possibilities of this form of critical engagement in areas that were not part of what Saussure had looked at initially.

In literary and cultural studies, structuralism paved the way for new approaches to reading texts, employing taxonomies for the extension of the possibilities of analysing the embedded processes therein. Writing in 1973, Robert Scholes offered the following perspective on the significance of 'Structuralist Criticism': 'I am convinced that the whole enterprise is not only sound but essential, that useful work will be done and is currently being done under the structuralist aegis' (135). In his examination of the Formalist study of literary texts, Scholes highlights the work of the Russian and Prague Schools which focussed on the relevance of the study of 'form' or 'structure' through an engaging assessment of historical parameters. Interestingly, in his widely-circulated study of the structuralist and Formalist enterprise, Fredric Jameson took a different view, situating the process as a 'prison-house', thereby shifting the focus onto its limitations as a critical method in literary studies.

It is imperative to see the interconnections between the linguistic emphasis in structuralist criticism – that closely borders on formal analysis – and the reading of literary texts as a composite of language components in Formalism, because developments in subsequent theory offered to extend the mode of reading beyond such a frame. In the years leading up to the primarily French intervention in critical theory in the 1960s and 70s, where the re-assessment of structuralism took place, it is evident that the path paved by the works of Saussure, Levi-Strauss and Roman Jakobson, for example, facilitated a more intensive conditioning of the questions involved in the reading process which were then taken up by poststructuralist thinkers and writers.

In the field of cultural studies, Roland Barthes was one of the earliest French critics to take up the possibilities of the sign as an enabling agency for the study of situations that were not conventionally considered part of the textualised literary space. In two of his early books, *Mythologies* (1957) and *Elements of Semiology* (1964), Barthes offered a systematic road map for the study of cultural structures through an engagement with the sign as the pathway to meaning-making. In *The Fashion System* (1967) he extended the reading process to look at the world of haute couture by examining the 'system' structurally: 'My main intention has been to reconstitute step by step a system of meaning, in a more or less immediate manner, that is with least possible recourse to external objects, even to those of linguistics, whose use here is admittedly frequent but always elementary' (*The Fashion System* x).

A little prior to this, Barthes stated that the 'object of this inquiry is structural analysis of women's clothing as currently described by Fashion magazines; its method was originally inspired by the general science of signs postulated by Saussure under the name *semiology*' (ix). It is evident that by the middle of the twentieth century the structuralist poetics envisioned by Saussure with regard to the study of language and its formation and function expanded its impact beyond the immediate field of linguistics and accommodated areas that were conventionally seen as belonging to culture and society. Along with literary studies, it was the fields of anthropology and culture that drew on the insights of what came to be placed under the rubric of structuralism. These, however, were not the only areas that acknowledged what the Saussurean frame had to offer in studies such as psychology, sociology, and psychoanalysis. Such a wide-ranging engagement of the feasibility of the structuralist paradigm attested to the significance and relevance of the Saussurean model for the investigation into issues which were not looked at from this perspective.

The Limits of Structuralism

With the extension of structuralism as a viable study-model for the fields of language, society and culture beginning to impact different disciplines, questions also began to emerge about the limitations of such an enterprise in the writings and thought of many analysts in the second half of the twentieth century. An interesting facet of this process can be seen in writings of Roland Barthes who, in the second phase of his career, made the transition from being a structuralist thinker to one who came to occupy that space which housed the poststructuralists. In a path-breaking essay titled 'From Work to Text' (1971) Barthes provides his perspective on the limitations of the structuralist approach to the reading of texts thus:

> The Text can be approached, experienced, in reaction to the sign. The work closes on a signified. There are two modes of signification which can be attributed to this signified: either it is claimed to be evident and the work is then the object of a literal science, of philology, or else it is considered to be secret, ultimate, something to be sought out, and the work then falls under the scope of a hermeneutics, of an interpretation (Marxist, psychoanalytic, thematic, etc.); in short, the work itself functions as a general sign and it is normal that it should represent an institutional category of the civilization of the Sign. The Text, on the contrary, practises the infinite deferment of the signified, is dilatory; its field is that of the signifier and the signifier must not be conceived of as "the first stage of meaning", its material vestibule, but, in complete opposition to this, as its deferred action. (*Image, Music, Text* 158)

The Saussurean format consisting of the signifier–signified paradigm is here shown to be limiting in terms of what textuality entails when read in terms of the deferment that takes place in the meaning-assigning process. Barthes points out that a text does not submit itself to a fixed or closed meaning, even though the structuralist approach seems to suggest so when it comes to reading the process of signification. In his view, Barthes suggests, the situating of the signifier as the agency facilitating the 'first stage of meaning' does not do justice to the process of deferral that is inherently the property of reading the textual sign. The closure that is insisted upon by the Saussurean engagement of signs is seen as a limitation in the study and reading of texts by critics such as Barthes. What it also brought into the ambit of analysis is the understanding that a text does not merely occupy the realm of signification, having nothing to do beyond its signifier–signified axis, but that the process is very complex and to see it as self-enclosed would be a form of reduction.

Fredric Jameson locates a similar tendency when he examines the system foregrounded by Saussure: 'the basic problem of the idea of system remains after we make abstraction of the purely material substratum: if substances no longer exist in the ordinary sense, then how can relationships function, of what and in what does value consist?' (16–17). The argument here draws attention to the relationship between the constituents within the system of signs which presumes, in Jameson's view, that the operative logic is self-sufficient and does not accommodate the possibilities of taking it beyond what the relation itself points to. This is seen as a form of insularity which does not permit engaging in an interpretive process outside of the system of signs. The structuralist approach thereby seems to close down the possibilities of reading texts, including cultural and literary, outside what the signifier–signified relation offers through its space of signification. This sense of closure is thus opened up for criticism as a limiting condition in the manner of the process of definition. Jameson looks to invite attention to this mechanism as a vital condition of the limitations that structuralism subjects itself to when he states, 'The point is that for Saussure ... the basic components of the system, are somewhat self-defining: inasmuch as they are themselves, whatever they may turn out to be, the basic units of meaning, it is logically impossible to go beyond them and to work out some more abstract definition in terms of which they would function as members of a class' (17).

Thus critically situated, the limitations of structuralism appear more stark, more so because the principles with which Saussure started his enterprise of analysis with respect to language and its formation were systematised to attend to the ramifications of the process of signification. When the extension of the structuralist premise to fields outside the domain of language took place, it was tailored to address the feasibility of examining structures in those particular areas. Anthropology, for instance, saw a working out of the conditions of reading societal formations and patterns when Claude Levi-Strauss engaged the Saussurean dimension to envisage the possibilities of such an exercise. The phrase, 'structural anthropology' – not just the name of the book he articulated his argument in, but the very sense of design in the approach – stuck and came to represent the *idea* of structuralism beyond its immediate field.

When Jacques Derrida argued for a more open-ended approach towards the question of knowledge production, he focused on the limitations of the binary structure that Levi-Strauss grounded his thesis about customs upon, a process which placed the entire structuralist engagement under scrutiny. Derrida, and subsequent critics who came to be identified with the poststructuralist process, argued that the reliance on a binary structure had serious limitations with respect to the nature of meaning and knowledge.

How can this line of questioning be seen in the context of the limitations of structuralism? To start with, Saussure did not specifically argue that the signification process would lead to or could be applied to an opening up of modes of reading texts beyond the nature of language-meaning. Also, historicity and cultural difference emerged as important points in newer reading schemes which needed to be approached, not in isolation but in terms of a critical engagement that would extend well beyond its immediate structural frame. Such critique thus opened up the bound frame of the structuralist argument into a wider space where 'closure' was seen as a limiting format. The view that some form of either/or structure was at work when structuralists approached their subject, rendered the binary as a *given*; a kind of foundation upon which the premise of the subsequent argument was placed.

The understanding that a set of mutually exclusive signifiers operated to condition the very nature of knowledge construction constituted the critical approach against it, primarily because it was seen as something that prevented the examination of situations outside such a duality-based structure. The placement of this opposition/binary as one of the basic characteristics of the structuralist approach was seen as a reduction of its terms of reference. What it entailed, in effect, was that questions engendered by situations beyond these binaries remained outside the purview of structuralist studies. In a way, structuralism could be seen as a kind of Procrustean bed which facilitated the reading of language, society and culture, but in a reduced, restricted environment where alternatives and variations in discourse could not be accommodated or addressed. This implied that evolving situations in any of the areas that were approached from the structuralist perspective remained outside the purview of analysis.

The structuralist focus on the interrelations between things, including language units, was espoused by linguists and cultural theorists where different possibilities of understanding were explored. However, poststructuralist thinkers saw this emphasis on the relational dimension as a place from which new and emerging aspects could not be accessed or dealt with. In other words, structuralism came to be seen as a straitjacket that did not foster critical reading beyond a point, but rather, reduced texts to a given predetermined frame, examined primarily through their relational potential. Such reductive framing of the subject can be limiting as an analytical exercise.

An example of reading without restrictive framing can be seen in Jacques Derrida's assessment of the nature of singularity, where he argues that a signature is both same and different at the same time. He calls it the condition of iterability. Such an envisioning of the signature would not have been feasible within the closed relational situation of the structuralist design as a determined format forms one of its fundamental arcs. In a discussion with Peter Eisenman, Jacques Derrida argues that sameness and difference coexist but with a singularity that remains fluid and situated when it is about the signature:

A signature must be unique; it must be repeated as the same but each time is different. Each time I sign a cheque it is a different signature but it is the same. It is the possibility of being the same while being different. Iterability is the condition of possibility of any identity, any uniqueness, which inscribes a difference within absolute uniqueness. (Derrida 19)

When it comes to conceptual questions that demand scrutiny outside relational frames, the structuralist orientation appears limiting as a critical exercise. A wide range of literary and cultural issues came to be examined in the 1960s and the following decades for which structuralism was found wanting as an analytical mode. Michel Foucault's arguments regarding the configuration and enunciation of madness, for instance, demonstrates the limitations of sticking to a relational frame in the context of the fluidity involved in such discourses. 'Madness', he argues, consists of

... subjecting an utterance, which appears to conform to the accepted code, to another code whose key is contained within that same utterance so that this utterance becomes divided within itself. It says what it says, but it adds a silent surplus that quietly enunciates what it says and according to which code it says what it says. This is not the case of an encoded language but of one that is structurally esoteric. That is to say, it does not communicate a forbidden meaning by concealing its meaning; it positions itself from the start in an essential fold of the utterance. A fold that hollows it out from within and perhaps to infinity. Therefore it matters little what is said in such a language and what meaning is being delivered there. It is this obscure and central liberation at the very heart of the utterance, its uncontrollable flight toward a source that is always without light, that no culture can readily accept. Such utterance is transgressive not in its meaning, not in its verbal property, but in its *play*. ('Madness, the Absence of Work' 294)

When we look at the argument put forward by Foucault, it is evident that the closed signifier–signified structure that serves the structuralists in examining language, society and culture would be inadequate as a paradigm for the study of situations that entail a more nuanced reading of the terms involved in something such as madness or the functioning of signature. In the quote from Foucault above, there is the reference to play, a condition that is embedded in the very making and circulation of the discourse of madness, such an envisioning of social tropes and cultural situations cannot be sufficiently addressed through the aegis of structuralism.

The poetics of structuralism limits the meaning-making process to a closed, settled condition, irrespective of the circumstances that may evolve in specific contexts and are marked with an open-endedness which cannot be accommodated through a signifier–signified equation. Many poststructuralist thinkers, spread across disciplines and fields, have drawn attention to the limiting frame of a sign-centric agency. The societal features that Levi-Strauss drew out in his minutely structured analyses bear considerable relevance in the context of social and cultural anthropology. Many thinkers have developed his insights and taken his mode of reading mode to expand the horizons of the discipline further. In these particular reading contexts, the structuralist approach facilitated by the pioneering work of Levi-Strauss has broken unprecedented ground, offering a framework for elaboration and subsequent analysis.

What has changed, ever since the poststructuralist intervention from the 1960s onwards, has been the focus on the inherent fault lines that are embedded in the constituted 'structures' which Levi-Strauss took for granted as he embarked on his investigations. In settling upon a series of 'givens' – taken-for-granted assumptions – Levi-Strauss built the edifice of social structure on a solidity that came to be challenged for what it entailed. In this context we can consider Levi-Strauss's argument regarding the efficacy of following a sociological perspective, which he claims possesses its own truth-value primarily because it has an almost unassailable position as a given. In discussing Edward Westermarck's methodological approach to the study of societies, Levi-Strauss is categorical in his preference of sociology over biology as a mode of enquiry. *Structural Anthropology Zero*, where the following passage appears, crystallises some of his fundamental structuralist arguments, clearly framing critical assumptions which he believed would serve the enquirer most effectively in the pursuit of knowledge about human societies:

> [I]f well founded, [Westermarck's theory of marriage] confers on sociology a scientific status as eminent as that of

biology, and perhaps even more so. For if social institutions are, as Westermarck thinks, based on instinct, they become explainable insofar as we can connect the former to the latter. Yet the sociologist is better placed than the biologist to do so, for the latter is entirely ignorant of the causes of organic variations presupposed by natural selection. On the contrary, the causes of social phenomena are accessible. The sociological method is thus the appropriate method for discovering the causes of social phenomena. (Levi-Strauss 68)

Poststructuralist interventions that cut through such solidified and grounded assumptions not only sounded the limits of structuralist inquiry, but also facilitated a more open critical enterprise. The crumbling of these givens unsettled the structuralist world view, rendering unstable the very foundations structuralism stood upon. Thinkers such as Jacques Derrida and Paul de Man pointed out the fluidity involved in the whole exercise, where conditions were taken for granted insofar as they were assumed to be valid but became untenable once the structuralist design's assurance turned out to be not as valid. With emerging areas that required intervention, it was the growing incompatibility of the structuralist paradigm with evolving ideas that took a critical turn which brought about the advent of the reading frames subsequently identified with poststructuralism.

THE ADVENT OF POSTSTRUCTURALISM

Poststructuralism did not emerge with any suddenness but was in the process of becoming in the late 1950s when the structuralist appropriation of cultural forms and matrices found the Saussurean paradigm to be strained to its limits. For instance, Roland Barthes's configuration of 'mythic' structures in the modern context bore, among its many potential possibilities, the questioning of the terms of taken-for-granted realities. Human understanding and meaning-making are governed by certain terms of reference or codes to which a society subscribes at a given time. In *Mythologies*, Barthes proposed a reorientation of these terms of reference. By the time critics such as Barthes began exploring modes of engaging with realities other than the lettered text, the efficacy of Saussurean linguistics had come to be established – a process which enabled structuralism to expand its frontiers as a meaning-enabling agency beyond language into fields such as anthropology and cultural studies. Such expansion of this critical model, however, also opened up the fault lines in the reading process, bringing into question the extent to which the structuralist paradigm could be engaged with in approaching complex social and cultural phenomena. Barthes is not the only one who hovered on the frontiers when it came to the structuralist mode of understanding/explaining knowledge-processing, but did not directly move towards its questioning.

What Barthes engaged with in *Mythologies*, for instance (which is often situated as a form of the structuralist engagement with cultural studies), was a break from the limiting purview of the text-centric analysis that occupied literary criticism, especially in the Anglo-American context. Seen through such a frame, structuralism offered the possibility of challenging the literary-only dimensions of critical reading by positing a form of engagement that would open up the critical world to newer ways of looking at texts. Placing this aspect in context, Craig Lundy states,

> Structuralism, as such, was an eminently modern movement that sought to break away from previous academic constraints by entirely recasting the terms and conditions for understanding human existence. Central to this intellectual revolution was the quest for scientificity. Due to its strong affiliation with science and scientific method, early structuralism was able to radically distinguish itself from traditional approaches to society in the humanities and consequently position itself between (if not above) the sciences and the arts. (Lundy 70)

There is merit in situating structuralism as a formulaic proposition where the argument is directed towards a meaning-making process that is self-sustained and operational within the signification structure involved it is involved with. In such a context, Lundy's placement of structuralism as methodically-oriented design that approximates the aspiration of a certain scientific engagement, makes historical sense. However, it is this singular marking of the knowledge space by a set matrix – in the context of structuralism it is the sign – which restricts it from addressing issues beyond the immediately signifying chain. Mid-twentieth century critical movements recognised the limits of structuralism, as the frontiers of cultural and literary studies expanded in ways that could not be accommodated by the singular focus of the sign as the agency through which knowledge was to be approached.

It is imperative, however, to look at the dissipation of the critical energies of structuralism not as a facilitation of what came to be known as poststructuralism in terms of a replacement model, but as a condition that saw the coming together of a variety of threads from different disciplines and contexts. As such, in addressing the question of poststructuralist thought or thinkers connected to it, it is necessary to recognise that no conscious or ready formulation under such a head was done. The prefix 'post', indicative of the aftermath of structuralism as an analytical agency, by association came to serve as the designation through which the critical environment of the 1960s and the subsequent decades could be accessed. Benoît Dillet sums up this situation succinctly:

> Poststructuralism as such does not exist. No group of philosophers or scholars ever formed a group called "poststructuralism", but what exists is "poststructuralism" as a retrospective epistemological construction that gives a point of meaning in the vast land-scape of 'French' philosophy. Although they have certainly not invented the term, Fredric Jameson, Gayatri Chakravorty Spivak, Jonathan Culler among other North American scholars were probably at the origin of this retrospective construction in the late 1970s and earlier 1980s. Poststructuralism is here, and its effects on research in social sciences and humanities have been tremendous. In fact, the reception of poststructuralism in political studies has been conditioned by the ways key poststructuralist authors (Hélène Cixous, Gilles Deleuze, Jacques Derrida, Michel Foucault, Félix Guattari, Luce Irigaray, Jean-François Lyotard) were read and classified or compartmentalised. (517)

Such a mapping brings to the fore the engagement of critics and thinkers with a process of examination where the frontiers of enquiry were not simply directed towards pitting one set of meanings against another, but a shift in the very nature of critical orientation itself. New Criticism, for instance, had located in the text the genesis of the enterprise, invigorating criticism with a process of reading where the prevalence of certain textual parameters were taken for granted. By the time the questioning of the efficacy of the structuralist mode began to consolidate, there was a movement towards engaging with issues of a more conceptual nature and it is this marking of the conceptual and ideational sites that occupied centre stage in the later decades of the twentieth century.

When Jacques Derrida proposed that the sign was not as secure as it seemed during the heyday of structuralism in his now-classic essay, 'Structure, Sign, and Play in the Discourse in the History of the Human Sciences', he did not just place the operational issues associated with the process of signification at the forefront of his argument. He actually went on to argue that the very edifice of the knowledge-making enterprise was fraught with complications that were not envisaged as such. This indicated a shift in the mode of engagement in literary and cultural studies, even though the thinkers now usually placed under the poststructuralist rubric did not quite deal with literature or cultural texts directly.

Such intervention took place on multiple fronts and not necessarily in conjunction with one another. Traditional philosophy departments came to see people such as Derrida and Foucault as outsiders who disturbed the thought-trajectory that moved ahead with the continuum, the philosophical analyses moving along set frames. What these thinkers, now retrospectively seen as poststructuralists, did was to de-situate the norms of enquiry, inaugurating a series of questioning formats that came to unsettle conventions across disciplines. Whether it was Luce Irigaray with the question of identity and gender relations or Foucault with the discursive turn with respect to knowledge production, the frames of critical reference altered quite significantly. Irigaray and Foucault are instances of a phenomenal shift in orientation that came to impact a wide range of issues across the academic world, including those that had a recognisable 'tradition' in terms of disciplinary history. The shift was not merely a matter of another proposition that sought to relook at the limiting dimensions of structuralism, but a major reorientation in the space of critical theory.

What this entailed was the opening up of the fields of literary and cultural studies, making way for insights that were not from existing formats of 'literature' but a wide variety of intellectual positions. This can also be seen in terms of the examination of issues that were conceptually driven: language, knowledge, reality, truth, subjectivity, gender, system, materiality, modes of access, technology, space, narrativity – some of the focal areas that came to occupy the minds of thinkers who argued in different ways about how to address them.

One of the issues that came to be questioned was 'totalisation', or the tendency to take situations and positions for granted. Whether it was New Criticism or structuralism, it was assumed that meaning was not only accessible, but also worth pursuing. This perspective was eventually given short shrift by the re-framing of critical priorities by thinkers such as Foucault and Derrida, as has been briefly discussed above. In *The Order of Things* – to take this point through an example of this reorientation – Foucault examines the process of 'classification', a structuring programme evident across disciplines from the systematic study of language to the botanical analysis of plant life. Foucault argues that in placing the prevalent method of systematic study in a field within a set frame, a 'discourse' came to be developed and 'knowledge' found validity through its transcription in 'language': 'By limiting and filtering the visible, structure enables it to be transcribed into language. It permits the visibility of the animal or plant to pass over in its entirety into the discourse that receives it' (*The Order of Things* 147).

The key Foucauldian terms – discourse and knowledge – find their operative value in this citation, but more than their presence as terms, it is the dissipation of the conventions of enquiry that is so significant here. No longer is knowledge a *given* to be accessed as something outside of the pursuit of a certain subject, and discourse is that which frees the frontiers of historical understanding from the straitjacket of chronology and reliable narrativity. In his 'Preface to the English Edition', Foucault presents a map of his objective:

> Frontiers are redrawn and things usually far apart are brought closer, and vice versa: instead of relating the biological taxonomies to other knowledge of the living being (the theory

of germination, or the physiology of animal movement, or the statics of plants), I have compared them with what might have been said at the same time about linguistic signs, the formation of general ideas, the language of action, the hierarchy of needs, and the exchange of goods. (*The Order of Things* x–xii)

When it was first published in 1966, *The Order of Things* inaugurated a critical paradigm that asked the enquirer a set of questions which redrew the board. It placed things not along a linear thought process, but on a plane where the coexistence of apparently unconnected frames of reference came to occupy spaces of importance. What Foucault did was to open up the critical space so as to facilitate different approaches to the subject under enquiry. Instead of a linear and conventional causal movement where things were expected to fall into place, Foucault sought to invest in the inquiring mechanism itself a more opened up space, and it subsequently came to impact the ways in which critical enquiry was processed and embarked upon. In effect, what emerged in this Foucauldian enterprise – over a series of books extending up to *Technologies of the Self* – was the relevance of an 'archaeology of knowledge'; a form of epistemic investigation that firmly eschewed skimming the surface to arrive at meaning. There were other debates as well that contributed to the re-forming of the paradigms of knowledge and meaning. For instance, following the publication of 'Death of the Author' by Roland Barthes in 1968, Foucault did not shy away from criticising his French contemporary when he offered a variant of the same issue in 'What is an Author?'. This is just one example where, within the engagement with questions of knowledge, there remained room for locating oneself differently from other critical interventions.

Poststructuralism, looked at the question of authority critically, bringing to the fore the idea of knowledge being part of a mode of processing, not an absolute given. Such a positioning of direction in terms of how enquiry was to be marked opened up space for other questions to emerge. This is how in the 1960s and 1970s, poststructuralism emerged as a viable critical process: not one consolidated model of investigation but a congeries of modes surfacing from different centres of enquiry. By the end of the

1970s, two interesting books, for instance, signalled this emergence by drawing on how criticism could no longer be done through the reality or truth-pursuing formats such as New Criticism or structuralism. One is *Critical Practice* by Catherine Belsey and the other *Is There a Text in this Class?* by Stanley Fish; both forging new ground, both spin-offs from this very critical environment. Within a decade, poststructuralism began to make its impact felt across the Anglo-American classroom, to which there was not only a guarded response, but also evident resistance.

THE PATH TO CONTEMPORARY LITERARY AND CULTURAL STUDIES

The critical interventions brought about by insights from thinkers such as Derrida, Foucault, Irigaray and others who moved beyond the structure–meaning axis, worked gradually towards unsettling the 'conventions' of looking at literature and culture. Conventions in literary and cultural studies are usually engaged with and re-situated in terms of the reading practices that make their mark in a given age, but the poststructuralist moves enabled a more definitive shift away from the locus of meaning; something that had not necessarily been questioned so critically before. When Barthes examined the textuality of the Book of Genesis for example, or the cinematic dimensions of media in culture, such reading procedures opened up the 'text' from the critical exigencies that bound it in the modernist phase. The view – part of a critical jettisoning of theory – that poststructuralism facilitated a free-float of analytical apparatuses stemmed from the fact that these critical interventions contested the sense of certainty that was taken for granted in a given argument. Many of these questioning processes emerged from France, and thinkers such as Foucault, Derrida, Lacan, Barthes, Cixous and Althusser examined, within their own brackets, forms of conceptualisation that considerably impacted literary and cultural studies.

Yet poststructuralism was not merely a French phenomenon. The translations of the writings of the Russian thinker Mikhail Bakhtin and his circle, for instance, opened up new ways of looking at narrative fiction, and concepts such as polyphony and heteroglossia enabled access to cultures of writing by looking at possibilities that were not explored earlier. Bakhtin's work formed part of the Formalist School in Russian literary scholarship during a time when the New Critics were plying their brand of criticism in America. Yet, in the first half of the twentieth century, Bakhtin was virtually unheard of in the English-speaking world. In his assessment of the arrival of Bakhtin onto the critical scene, David Lodge argued that criticism could not simply be a meaning-seeking exercise after the Russian theorist had demonstrated the significance of dialogism in the reading of fiction. David Lodge's *After Bakhtin* marks a major accommodation of the perspective that critical convention consolidated through the agency of New Criticism would no longer be adequate in the reading of fiction. Likewise, while placing Argentinian writer and thinker Jorge Luis Borges in a matrix where poststructuralist openness is markedly present, we see how contemporary reading practices can locate certain aspects in a modernist writer which early criticism did not quite address. Take the following argument where the Borgesian world is looked at through the lens of différance, a reading that would not have been considered feasible in the time of New Criticism:

> Laying the groundwork for deconstructionism and as prototypes thereof, most of Borges' fictions, "Menard" in particular, in a sense, put on display what Derrida calls *différance* – deferring meaning construction to different people across time and space. Accordingly, Benjamin's concept of afterlife, related to his search for the realization of pure language through translation, in one way or another echoes Borges' view of the literary work. (Rasool and Hossein 2)

The Borgesian text affords a kind of critical engagement that a concept such as différance takes as part of its critical space. More than that, it is the reorientation brought about by this exercise which opens up reading practice beyond the limits of New Criticism and structuralism. In examining texts that are not considered to be traditionally aligned to the world of literature, these thinkers looked at conceptual structures and examined how they were significant in terms of the ways in which questions of knowledge and reality came to operate in critical discourse. The Freudian mode of looking at the subject and unsettling the stability of the 'self' had already opened up fissures in engaging with the knowledge question vis-à-vis the issue of subjectivity in the early twentieth century. When Jacques Lacan began his seminars, he extended Freudian agency to look at layers that were not accessible in the theoretical models of psychoanalytic criticism previously, combining Saussurean insights with those from Roman Jakobson and reorienting structuralism to address the complex nature of the human subject: a process which uniquely places the Lacanian exercise beyond the recognised formativity of the signifier–signified axis.

In an interesting debate, Derrida brought the poststructuralist argument to a head when he took on the Lacanian reading of Poe's 'The Purloined Letter' in 'The Purveyor of Truth'. The fact that the question of 'truth' came to occupy such a significant place in the wake of the critiques of the structuralist formatting of knowledge is evidenced by this debate between Lacan and Derrida where the provisionality and relativity of the reading position emerged as a factor worth considering. The Lacanian argument, however, does not dis-embed the possibilities of engaging with cultural realities through the psychoanalytic frame. That psychoanalytic criticism has come to serve a wide variety of reading formats beyond its immediate conventional domain attests to the configurative elasticity of not just this agency, but of poststructuralism itself. Ian Parker marks the need to re-frame the markers through which psychoanalytic reading practices have come to impact the study of culture in contemporary criticism, when he delineates that 'psychoanalysis' is,

1. not only "about" psychoanalysis, but working within psychoanalytic reasoning, inhabiting it and turning it into a form of cultural critique;

2. not taking psychoanalysis as a privileged system of knowledge which comes from the outside and unlocks the secrets of culture, but recognizing psychoanalysis as embedded in the culture;

3. not treating psychoanalysis as a mysterious metanarrative but treating it as an historically material product and resource, as the tool and result of critical inquiry;

4. not treating psychoanalysis as a disconnected expert system but as a form of narrative that is accessible to, and accessed by the selves created by it;

5. not treating psychoanalysis simply as a clinical practice devoted to the amelioration of symptoms, but as a system of symptoms which is structured by and which structures culture. (Parker 303)

By the 1980s, it became evident that the many reading positions which were brought forth by critics such as Derrida, Foucault, Cixous, Althusser and Lacan, among others, moved well beyond the exegetical frames in which they were placed, and this extension came to be seen as part of the process of doing criticism, both literary and cultural.

The centrality of meaning and the quest for its recovery, however, was not something that could be bypassed just because poststructuralism arrived – this was the contention of those who stood by the value of a critical practice where the conventions of textual understanding were considered valid and relevant. One of the mis-readings of the exercises that many poststructuralist thinkers located their works through, was the view that literature could not be abandoned to the whims of any relativist agency, leaving the question of 'interpretation' hanging in limbo. In his essay 'Is There a Text in This Class?' Stanley Fish sought to broker a middle path by recognising the presence of the condition of indeterminacy on the one hand and belief on the other. The forging of this kind of literary criticism, especially in the context of what it brought to the classroom scene, shows how poststructuralism could not simply be wished away. It may seem accommodative in terms of its framing, but it is more significantly a recognition that literary criticism could not be unresponsive to the ways in which critical debates were raging 'outside' the field. This alertness can be seen in Fish's summation of the critical scene where he plays out the pedagogic as well as the intellectual condition in terms of how it was in the late 1970s:

> ... while relativism is a position one can entertain, it is not a position one can occupy. No one can *be* a relativist, because no one can achieve the distance from his own beliefs and assumptions which would result in their being no more

authoritative *for him* than the beliefs and assumptions held by others, or, for that matter, the beliefs and assumptions he himself used to hold. . . . The point is that there is never a moment when one believes nothing, when consciousness is innocent of any and all categories of thought, and whatever categories of thought are operative at a given moment will serve as an undoubted ground. (Fish 319–20)

It is evident that Stanley Fish is commenting on the emerging changes that came to impact the field of literary studies in the 1970s – there are allusions to the debate that raged between Meyer Adams and those thinkers associated with 'indeterminacy' (Fish 305) – poststructuralism being in a state of engagement with academia which had not quite consolidated into the formation it came to be perceived as in the next two decades. Fish's own reading frame – Reader Response Criticism – was, in effect, a development that looked at the fluidity of the process of textual engagement, which was interesting, among other reasons, for the fact that it emerged in a climate where reading itself came to be seen as something beyond the conventional classroom meaning-elucidation format. The evocation of the personal, an increasingly contested space in subsequent decades, was also a sign of a transitional phase in literary studies where questions of indeterminacy began to mark out the critical space by infringing upon the stability of determinate readings usually associated with structuralist poetics.

The recognition that a consummate theoretical model would suffice to look at literature and cultural studies thus came to be challenged once the structuralist inadequacy was highlighted by these various developments across disciplines. As John Frow points out, the fault lines that were present brought to the fore many other issues about discipline and method:

> [It] is not possible to contemplate redeeming a sense of disciplinary wholeness and purpose by means of a theoretical programme. Indeed, disciplinary coherence may not after all be as desirable a goal as the alternative values of theoretical openness and heuristic richness, It may be that the category of the literary itself is an obstacle both to the formation of a systematic knowledge of texts, and to that interdisciplinary dynamic and that sense of exploratory creativity that has

characterized literary studies at its best in the decades since the "moment of theory". (Frow 55)

Frow's argument places in context the nature of the 'exploratory creativity' that came to occupy different fields of study, emerging as it did from a variety of registers across multiple planes. What now seems like a consolidation of these critical energies, however, was not a formation designed at any stage to unsettle the programmatic dimensions of New Criticism or structuralism. Such moves are fluid interfaces that are also responses to the nature of thought-markers in contemporary society and culture, and the fields of literature and culture opening up to these insights attest to the increasingly fascinating dynamics that suggest the elasticity of the critical exercise.

REFERENCES

Barthes, Ronald. *Image, Music, Text*. Translated by Stephen Heath, Fontana, 1977.

---. *The Fashion System*. Translated by Matthew Ward and Richard Howard, U of California P, 1990.

Dillet, Benoît. "What is Poststructuralism?". *Political Studies Review*, vol. 15, no. 4, 2017, pp. 516–27.

Derrida, Jacques and Peter Eisenman. "Talking about Writing". *Any: Architecture New York*, May/June 1993, pp. 18–21.

Fish, Stanley. *Is There a Text in this Class?: The Authority of Interpretive Communities*. Harvard UP, 1980.

Foucault, Michel. "Madness, the Absence of Work". Translated by Peter Stastny and Deniz Şengel, *Critical Inquiry*, vol. 21, no. 2, 1995, pp. 290–98.

---. *The Order of Things*. Translated by A.M. Sheridan, Routledge, 2002.

Frow, John. "On Literature in Cultural Studies". *The Aesthetics of Cultural Studies*, edited by Michael Berube, Blackwell, 2005.

Howarth, David R. *Poststructuralism and After: Structure, Subjectivity and Power*. Palgrave, 2013.

Jameson, Fredric. *The Prison-house of Language: A Critical Account of Structuralism and Russian Formalism*. Princeton UP, 1972.

Katz, Joseph T. "Saussure at Play and his Structuralist and Post-Structuralist Interpreters". *Cahiers Ferdinand de Saussure*, no. 68, 2015, pp. 113–32.

Levi-Strauss, Claude. *Structural Anthropology*. Translated by Claire Jacobson and Brooke Grundfest Schoepf, Basic Books, 1963.

---. *Structural Anthropology Zero*. Translated by Ninon Vinsonneau and Jonathan Magidoff, edited by Vincent Debaene, Polity, 2022.

Lundy, Craig. "From Structuralism to Poststructuralism". *The Edinburgh Companion to Poststructuralism*, edited by Benoît Dillet, Iain MacKenzie and Robert Porter, Edinburgh UP, 2013, pp. 69–94.

Parker, Ian. "Psychoanalytic Narratives: Writing the Self into Contemporary Cultural Phenomena". *Narrative Inquiry*, vol. 13, no. 2, pp. 301–15.

Rabaté, Jean-Michel. Introduction. *Structuralism*, by John Sturrock, Blackwell, 2003, pp. 1–16.

Rasool, Moradi Joz and Hossein, Pirnajmuddin. "Benjamin and Borges: Reflections on Afterlife and Translation". *Babel*, vol. 64, no. 1, 2018, pp. 1–18.

Saussure, Ferdinand de. *Course in General Linguistics*. Translated by Wade Baskin, Philosophical Library, 1959.

Scholes, Robert. "The Contributions of Formalism and Structuralism to the Theory of Fiction". *Novel: A Forum on Fiction*, vol. 6, no. 2, 1973, pp. 134–51.

Stawarska, Beata. *Saussure's Linguistics, Structuralism, and Phenomenology: The Course in General Linguistics after a Century*, Palgrave Macmillan, 2020.

Sturrock, John. *Structuralism*, Blackwell, 2003.

Chapter Five

The Challenge to 'Truth' and 'Reality'

QUESTIONING 'BASIC' ASSUMPTIONS

In looking at developments in critical practice in the twentieth century, we can see a move away from the text–meaning focus to one where a questioning of norms came to occupy the space of 'analysis'. Poststructuralism was not something that was merely a critical response to the space where meaning-making was taken to be one of the priorities of the reading enterprise. It was, more insistently, a form of questioning that took on existing patterns of engaging with thought. In effect, what was considered to be a given was now seen as being fraught with inherent fault lines and it was not a question of a different interpretation, but a re-examination of those assumptions which held sway and were taken for granted. Assessing the situation that emerged in the wake of the critique of structuralism in the 1960s, Robert Young maps it thus:

> [P]ost-structuralist thinkers, such as Derrida, Foucault and Lacan, have questioned the status of science itself, and the possibility of the objectivity of any language of description or analysis, as well as the assumptions implicit in the Saussurian model of linguistics on which structuralism may be said to be broadly based. The effect of this work on contemporary theories of criticism has been considerable. Recently, its impact has begun to extend towards criticism generally, affecting the way we think about literature and, more specifically, the way we read. (vii)

What does this questioning entail? How are we to look at the exercise of 'criticism' in this context where the very edifice of textuality is placed in an altogether new paradigm? One of the ways in which this can be located pertains to the nature of the field and what it operated as, especially in terms of the envisaged purpose of criticism. At the beginning of the twentieth century, criticism saw the placement of an emphasis on the centrality of the text with the dissociation of the 'author' serving as an important perspective in this process of evaluation. While critics like T.S. Eliot argued for an impersonal response to the text, there was the tacit implication that meaning was still accessible, provided a worthwhile reading apparatus was in place. Anglo-American literary criticism found itself embattled when the nuances involved in the reading of texts emerged as points of contention in debates that were centred on the validity of interpretation. Critics contested other reading positions in order to argue how their own frameworks would stand up to scrutiny against those fashioned by their rivals; so much so that we saw debates rage about Lady Macbeth's children or the implications of Ben Jonson's comic sense in a volatile society. A variety of interpretative positions sought to outsmart each other, and journals such as Leavis's *Scrutiny* provided a platform to play out their critical minutiae.

This text-centric, meaning-ascertaining mechanism held more sway following the popularity of 'close reading' as a technique advocated especially by the New Critics, and irrespective of the adoption of a formulaic mode involving conditions such as the locating of paradox or tension in texts, the critical exercise in academic disciplines tended to concentrate on the significance of a sustained textual reading engagement. Such a technique seemed to offer the critic and the reader the pedagogic wherewithal to make arguments within a recognised critical frame whereby it became feasible to present contestations and come out the better by using the framing effectively. Phrases such as 'dissociation of sensibility' – used by Eliot with a specific argument in mind – became buzzwords and promoted the relevance of one kind of reading over another. In such an intellectually oriented climate, what came to be seen as conceptual sparring retained the purpose and goal of meaning-seeking within its operative matrix. Across the critical space, people like F. R. Leavis or Cleanth Brooks, for instance, sought to argue for the need to engage with the text in order to interpret and understand literature. When Cleanth Brooks published *The Well-Wrought Urn* in the late 1940s, the idea that meaning is what is worthy of being pursued seemed to be one of his main arguments. This comes into focus when he looks at the role of the reader and orients the significance of meaning in the understanding of a text:

> We have to ask the reader to become acquainted with the poet's language (using the term in its broadest sense). But it is important to note what the reader is not asked to do. He is not asked to give up his own meanings or beliefs or to adopt permanently those of the poet. It will be sufficient if he will understand the unit meanings with which the poet begins – that is, that he understands the meanings of the words which the poet uses – and if he will so far suppress his convictions or prejudices as to see how the unit meanings or partial meanings are built into a total context. (Brooks 226)

The assumption – so succinctly articulated in this Brooks passage – that meaning is accessible was part of an intellectual climate where the process of reading was seen as an exercise that relied on a series of givens. That such taken-for-granted assumptions could be subjected to scrutiny came to the fore when the structuralist and Formalist modes appeared inadequate as 'tools' of interpretation, more so in the light of the increasing critique of these kinds of frameworks that came to be mounted in the 1960s.

The need to look at 'meaning' and 'interpretation' as areas associated with the dynamics of reading was not an early twentieth century phenomenon in literary criticism alone. It was a process that developed as part of a hermeneutical tradition, and though connected with the decoding of scripture, the analytical apparatus being invoked was not dissimilar to what literary criticism sought to pursue: to make sense of a text by an interpretational engagement with it. The difference in orientation is summed by cogently by Paul Ricoeur:

> For the interpreter, it is the text which has a multiple meaning; the problem of multiple meaning is posed for him only if what is being considered is a whole in which events, persons,

institutions, and natural or historical realities are articulated. It is an entire "economy", an entire signifying whole, which lends itself to the transfer of meaning from the historical to the spiritual level. In the entire medieval tradition of the multiple meanings of Scripture, it is through great wholes that the quadruple meaning is articulated.

Today this problem in multiple meaning is no longer simply the problem of exegesis in the biblical or even in the secular sense of the word; it is rather an interdisciplinary problem . . . (63)

What Ricoeur is marking out here is the changing dimensions of the question of text and interpretation. As he points out, in the exegetical process of pursuing one meaning over others, the privileging of one thread does not bring forward the issue of interdisciplinarity in literary and cultural studies. What emerges, in the context of the critique of the structuralist straitjacket, is a recognition that formulaic patterns would not suffice in approaching and assessing texts, and even where concepts are used to address textual circumstances, taken-for-granted assumptions cannot serve as the logical base for the scaffolding of the argument itself. It is in such a climate of the intellectual re-orientation of the critical process that argumentation and interpretation came to be revisited, resulting in a questioning of the givens that had served the purpose of close reading.

Among those who critically looked at the 'stable' structures being engaged with prior to the arrival of thinkers such as Derrida and Foucault, it was not so much a case of disagreement with a particular idea or a set of ideas but the understanding that certain assumptions such as 'truth' and 'reality' stood on grounds that did not require any archaeological probing. Foucault's assessment of the discursive processes at work opened up the space of critical theory where assumptive grounds were seen as inadequate in the process of enquiry. Both the Foucauldian and Derridean expositions moved in the direction of an articulation where the idea of a centre came to be seriously challenged. In 'Structure, Sign, and Play in the Discourse of the Human Sciences', Derrida argued that the over-reliance on the 'centre' in Western metaphysics consolidated the ground for any assumption – which came to be called the transcendental signified – in such a manner that it left little room for any enquiry regarding the ground itself. In this essay Derrida went on to critically engage with the fault lines which are inherently part of any given idea or concept, something which came under the rubric of 'deconstruction'. This brought to the fore the questioning of a common sense understanding of knowledge. This was also part of the inquiry mounted during the New Criticism phase, but the argument then was in favour of a more sustained approach to making meaning accessible.

In such a context, the questioning of taken-for-granted assumptions in the wake of developments in critical thought in the 1960s made it untenable to pursue the understanding that meaning deciphered through the application of a given theoretical apparatus would suffice so far as that frame was concerned. What poststructuralist developments entailed was a re-marking of the critical space through a shift in the very mode of enquiry where those assumptions which formed part of the exercise came to be questioned. Subsequently, the enquiry into these processes of conceptual engagement came to occupy the realm of criticism, with the term 'theory' being used as the accommodative space where argumentation could take place.

'Truth' and 'Reality' as Areas of Enquiry

Prior to the interventions made by poststructuralist thinkers, primarily from the 1960s onwards, 'reality' and 'truth' were not considered areas that required intensive scrutiny or investigation. It became evident with the new modes of thinking now directed at the subject, for instance, that it was no longer a question of situating one interpretation against another, with a particular argument being seen as better placed and more sustainable in that particular context. The shift was of a more radical kind.

In the writings of the French psychoanalyst Jacques Lacan, the idea of the 'real' came to be located as a slippery space – a construct which did not serve as the synonym for what was taken to be common sense reality. Why was it required to complicate the question of reality and posit it in terms of what is elusive and almost inaccessible? What Lacan brought to the poststructuralist table was fascinating in many ways. First, he drew on the Saussurean index of the structure but accessed it for the purpose of looking at the agency of the unconscious, engaging with the slippage that pointed towards the complex situation of the human subject as being no longer devisable through the frame of Cartesian subjectivity. The human subject, being so complexly marked in the matrices of the real, required a very different theoretical grammar for it to be accessed and made sense of. It is in this context that Lacan examines the feasibility of seeing the realm of the real in an altogether new frame. Commenting on this process, Catherine Belsey explains,

> In Lacan's account, the meanings that give us our sense of reality are always acquired from outside. We learn to mean from other people, from a language that exists before we are born into it or, in Lacan's terms, from the irreducible Otherness of the symbolic order. As the subjects we become by means of our subjection to the symbolic order, we gain access to social reality, but we leave behind the real of the human organism in its continuity with its surroundings. From now on language will always come between us and direct contact with the real. (5)

Among other things, the understanding that the real was not as it was taken to be previously came to be recognised as a significant move in critical theory. What it entailed was not a positing of one idea of the real against another, but a shift in responsiveness across disciplines whereby it became difficult to engage with the notion that reality was fixed and therefore not subject to examination. The psychoanalytic domain was now not merely a specialised space where a sense of the self was placed in a plane of critical reading – the move made by thinkers such as Lacan and Deleuze and Guattari, with the latter two offering an altogether different matrix – and in effect, it was no longer tenable to pursue the objective of locating meaning or knowledge through the agency of the neutrality of the text.

It is significant that this shift was not something that had to do with contesting interpretations but a re-engagement with the question of knowledge and reality from a very different conceptual paradigm. To place this point in context, we need to configure the historical dynamic involving responses to the idea of the text in the twentieth century. The New Critics and some contemporaneous thinkers of the time located in the text the site of the meaning-making process, and any interpretation that was placed in an argumentative, oppositional space would be seen, in such a critical environment, as one which could be teased out from the very matrices of that site of textuality. Meaning remained, such critics argued, within the realm of accessibility, provided the apparatus deployed was directed towards it adequately. However, such an argumentative frame increasingly came to be seen as both critically naïve and inadequate in the context of the changing circumstances in which texts were looked at across disciplines. When we look at texts in the context of the developments in poststructuralist thought, argued Paul de Man, it is not possible to have an innocuous knower/known interface. However valid or relevant an interpretation may appear when made from a given position, it cannot be assumed to stand for what it is constituted by. It is not a question of understanding; rather it is the inexhaustibility of interpretation/meaning that comes to the fore here. The sense of the real that comes through thus, is ingrained in the reading process and not something which stands independent of the position from which the situation is viewed. As such, as Paul de Man points out, the sense of knowledge of a text ends up being an act of determination, marked through the process of the engagement that circumscribes it. In this context, he states,

> Texts in time can be structured, and can be categorically understood. So the temporal is assimilated into other modes of consciousness. So when we say there are no valid texts, it means that no text can be exhausted, or saturated, or fully understood in terms of its own temporal category. There will be temporal or spatial aspects of a text; they will readily be apparent in a text, but they will not saturate.
>
> Your readings will always be overdetermined in the sense that you will end up with several more or less incompatible readings, or underdetermined in the sense that you don't even come near to what the meaning seems to be. So you are never quite there. (De Man 153)

If textual circumstances cannot be taken for what they seemingly entail, does it imply that no sense can be made of anything? Neither de Man nor Lacan argue that the real is in the realm of non-textualised space; what they posit is connected to how such notions – the real or truth are only two such givens, among others, that have been in circulation in critical spaces – have found currency without being subjected to critical examination. On the one hand, there is the issue of the consolidation of these notions, and on the other, it is the way they have found validity in argumentative spaces of theoretical determinations.

Structuralist engagements, for instance, rely considerably on the efficacy of the signifier–signified axis functioning the way it is assumed to do, and the meaning-making process is thereby built upon this edifice. What this entails was that while there was room for Saussurean ideas such as the 'arbitrariness of the sign', the eventual fixity that the realm of signification was cemented through did not leave much scope for textual manoeuvres. The saturation that de Man refers to, thus closes off the interpretive space, making it difficult to locate the shifts that form part of taken-for-granted assumptions such as the real and truth, to take two instances. It was also in the wake of the recognition that structuralism was increasingly becoming inadequate in terms of how certain questions/givens needed to be investigated, that the role of 'narrative' emerged in this critical space. The terminology, though the same as that which was used in the modernist phase, was now re-situated to engage with something that also was a form of questioning the ways in which things came to be seen through the process of narrativisation.

That reality is factored in through the agency of the narrative process occupied the critical space more and more insistently. How narrative as a literary and cultural process was seen to mark out the critical space can be seen in how it cut across disciplines and was no longer confined to the specialised study of language. Thinkers such as Hayden White argued how the process of emplotment served as the crucial agency through which the emergence of what was either taken to be or constituted as truth or reality in a given context. Hayden White is often termed a postmodern historian, but his contribution in engaging with the limited structural imperatives of the classical 'history is fact' paradigm is an important intervention in poststructuralist theory. He posits the argument that the historical text, conventionally seen as a 'truth-text', emerges in a distinctively narratorial plane. He points out that there is no denying the significance of the role played by narrativity in the representation of factual situations. In his path-breaking essay 'The Value of Narrativity in the Representation of Reality', White draws attention to the connection between the discursive nature of narrative and its orientation in culture, embedding, as it does, that text which is read as both real and true when presented as history:

> Narrative becomes a *problem* only when we wish to give to *real* events the *form* of story. It is because real events do not offer themselves as stories that their narrativization is so difficult. What is involved, then, in that finding of the "true story," that discovery of the "real story" within or behind the events that come to us in the chaotic form of "historical records"? What wish is enacted, what desire is gratified, by the fantasy that real events are properly represented when they can be shown to display the formal coherency of a story? In the enigma of this wish, this desire, we catch a glimpse of the cultural function of narrativizing discourse in general, an intimation of the psychological impulse behind the apparently universal need not only to narrate but to give to events an aspect of narrativity.
> (White 8)

It is not just the sense of truth that a historical text narrativises that is called out; more importantly, it is the understanding of representation as unalterable fact that is seriously challenged. White does not pit one version/narrative against another, nor does he argue about the efficacy of a set of interpretations. What he marks out is much more radical: history is, in this framing drawn out by White, oriented by the narrative process, and what we get as truth or reality are not independent of how this comes about when articulated and represented in the form of texts. The impact of what White proposed in the context of historical narratives has been extended across fields well beyond the one it emerged from. Testimonials for instance, which draw closely from personal experience, are substantially constituted by the subject's representation of truth and reality, for that is what grants such narratives a sense of authenticity.

The Challenge to 'Truth' and 'Reality' 83

Dominick LaCapra suggests that the lessons of contemporary historiography can enable us to look at the ways in which the authenticity structure is marked out in realistically-oriented texts which deal with trauma and loss. That the relationship between the experientially-induced text and the narrative process deployed for its representation cannot be simple is something which comes across strongly in this examination. It is equally noticeable that the recognition of this complex representational imperative cannot be subsumed by the structuralist model, inviting a consideration of the many-sided dimensions of the process which places the claims of truth and reality within the ambit of narrativity and its discursive potential. It is in this context that LaCapra observes,

> At the very least, the complex relation of narrative structures to truth claims might provide a different understanding of modern and postmodern realism (including what has been termed *traumatic realism*) wherein correspondence itself is not to be understood in terms of positivism and essentialism but as a metaphor that signifies a referential relation (or truth claim) that is more or less direct or indirect (probably generically more indirect in fiction than in historiography). Furthermore, one might maintain that truth claims coming from historiography, on the levels of both events and structures, maybe employed in the discussion and critique of art (including fiction) in a manner that is especially pressing with respect to extreme events that still particularly concern people at present. (14)

The complex interface between the personal and the reality of the experiences represented do not emerge as inauthentic, as LaCapra points out, but what has become insistently clear in the context of poststructuralist interventions is that the processes through which such experiences are narrativised are worth examining. It is the understanding that there is no neutral space where reality or truth can be accessible which underpins many of the critical arguments that have followed the critique of the structuralist approach to knowledge. It does not, however, imply that this examination is governed by some kind of a blanket mechanism that would apply across reading positions. In fact, the very provisionality that impinges on the critique of structure is what marks the developments in contemporary theory. It is also an acknowledgement that the same framework cannot suffice in engaging with questions as loaded as reality and truth.

Open-Endedness

As writing questioning the limits of the structuralist argument began to emerge consistently in the 1960s and 70s, it led to the view that what was being resisted was the idea of closure as part of the meaning-making process. The assumption that the realm of signification involving the signifier–signified axis was centred on an assured meaning may have been something which structuralism consolidated, but the call for openness in reading and interpreting was not quite there, except sporadically. Challenging certainty as being one of the prerequisites of the critical enterprise is often traced back to Nietzsche, whose maverick questioning of institutions of thought provided glaring instances of refusal to rest on any kind of centrally located meaning. In a passage in *The Will to Power*, to cite a classic Nietzsche phrasal turn, he states, 'There are no facts, everything is in flux, incomprehensible, elusive; what is relatively most enduring is – our opinions' (326). Open-endedness is not quite an anthem or a slogan of poststructuralism, nor is it a formulaic code used to suggest that the sense of closure that functions in the quest for meaning is a tool to be used for unlocking something. What the questioning of the idea of closure implies is a recognition of the possibilities of reading not just texts, but also concepts and ideas that bear multiple threads.

One interesting example in this regard can be seen in Judith Butler's engagement with the idea of gender, often a taken-for-granted term in certain forms of feminist theory. What Butler argues is significant in that she locates the assumptions behind a commonly held understanding of gender, which can form the framework for an investigation into the ramifications of its use. Butler shows how a 'structured' process needs to be re-visited, especially since gender as a category and as a notion has come to be seen as an all-encompassing term. In this context, Butler explicates,

> Indeed, gender theorists and philosophers do not reflect enough on the fact that "gender" is a foreign term in every

language other than English, which means that gender theory has a problem of translation at the core of its project. Indeed, in some parts of the world there is a resistance to the idea of gender precisely because it is foreign. . . . For instance, "gender" is not a term that Simone de Beauvoir used. . . . And yet, arguably, her own writings pointed the way toward the development of one strain of the philosophy of gender. Beauvoir argued in *The Second Sex* that one is not born a woman but rather becomes one. That formulation became the basis for the feminist theoretical distinction between sex, understood as a biological reality, and gender, understood as the cultural or social meanings that that biological reality assumes in a specific time and place. (2)

Butler points out how casually the term was taken and made use of in the 1970s and 80s when its argumentative force was deemed both necessary and contingent for feminist theory. The operative distinction between the terms 'sex' and 'gender' served the feminist theoretical space quite well, but the assumption's functionality was not quite brought under the scanner. Butler's drawing of the critical map with regards to these terms brings the necessity of addressing issues of terminology and its associated implications into sharp focus. The structured space into which gender came to be increasingly placed thus received attention from Butler; a process which invites us to attend to the importance of not taking even critically forceful concepts for granted. Such interventions mark out the imperative of keeping the critical space open, with the locations of classificatory distinctions being drawn into the process of examination as well.

The idea of openness is not something that is an accessory or a tool – what many thinkers, whose work is now seen through the poststructuralist lens, have done is to argue for the need to re-examine the modes of enquiry that had served the critical environment for so long. The resistance to closure is therefore a form of the acknowledgement of the limited purview of structures when it comes to engaging with ideas that are not confined to a single matrix. Even within disciplines there is a trapdoor of the functional given which, as Butler has shown in the case of 'gender', can consolidate and become encrusted without its forcefulness being impaired. It is in such a context that an alertness to the limitations of reductionism and closure needs to be considered. The cultivation of openness as a process is not argued for by any of these thinkers as the other of closure. Rather, the emergence of the significance of a wider accommodative frame that is provisional serves to facilitate critical agency more effectively than what structuralism did.

The Examination of 'Knowledge' as a Question

With the interventions of poststructuralism questioning the process through which 'knowledge' is accessed and conditioned for dissemination, the nature of the engagement with knowledge itself came under the scanner. The idea of knowledge did not occupy literary critics of the early twentieth century as a question of eminence, primarily because the focus was on the issue of interpretation and its correctness established through a chosen argumentative frame. As Jean-François Lyotard points out, the situation could no longer be looked at through the same lens nor in the same vein, for the very possibility of knowledge as a given required serious interrogation. More than that, the conventional view that knowing was part of a process of educative design or upbringing was not only imperilled, but also inadequate. That knowledge production is a matter of multiple conditions at play could no longer be ignored.

> The old principle that the acquisition of knowledge is indissociable from the training (*Bildung*) of minds, or even of individuals, is becoming obsolete and will become ever more so. The relationship of the suppliers and users of knowledge to the knowledge they supply and use is now tending, and will increasingly tend, to assume the form already taken by the relationship of commodity producers and consumers to the commodities they produce and consume — that is, the form of value. Knowledge is and will be produced in order to be sold, it is and will be consumed in order to be valorised in a new production: in both cases, the goal is exchange.
> (Lyotard 4)

The map laid out by Lyotard presents an elaborate critical apparatus for the engagement with the markers through which 'knowledge' is configured, and how the process is not easily summarised through a set of pre-structured registers. As is evident from the above passage, knowledge being a matter of acquisition, determined and controlled by the knower through training, is a limiting view as it restricts the parameters of engagement by means of a single agency. In effect, such a centrist approach to knowledge becomes increasingly untenable in the poststructuralist environment. Foucault approached this issue by looking at the significance of the episteme both as mode and as a site that needed to be considered, not as closed structured things but through its discursive potential, spread out across planes or fields not necessarily aligned or situated together. Associations are crucial in the determination of the framing process, which Foucault points towards when he looks at the relation between power and knowledge. The marking of this relational space is not a conditioned structure, but a fluid interweaving that plays out the nature of the push-and-pulls at work in a given situation. Foucault explains it thus:

> Now I have been trying to make visible the constant articulation I think there is of power on knowledge and of knowledge on power. We should not be content to say that power has a need for such-and-such a discovery, such-and-such a form of knowledge, but we should add that the exercise of power itself creates and causes to emerge new objects of knowledge and accumulates new bodies of information. (51)

Importantly, in the Foucauldian framing of the way knowledge is generated and functionalised, it is not something that operates independently of the process that draws it in. Knowledge operates through a network, a set of discourses, and the very notion that meaning or 'knowledge' is an independent entity ready to be discovered, comes to be scrutinised and re-situated in this new critical environment. The examples from Lyotard and Foucault are not the only ones that look at the issue of knowledge and its genealogy from a critical perspective that reflects the poststructuralist engagement with enquiry into taken-for-granted assumptions, but they are representative in that we get to see how the conventional approach to the idea of knowing is one which has come under insistent scrutiny. In order to see the point of departure, it is important to examine the conventional approach to the knowledge question, such as the one argued here by Ralph Monroe Eaton:

Meaning, for example, is present in all knowledge, from the simplest perception to the most complex mathematical expression. Any knowledge that does not make use of meaning is an immediate awareness, an intuition, which can give no rational account of itself. Just what *meaning* is, is a thorny question. But if a satisfactory answer can be given, the description of knowledge will have been pushed forward some distance. Moreover, one of the most notable facts about knowledge — and this is plainly connected with the presence of meaning — is that it can be expressed. Knowledge can be shut in between the covers of books and passed on from generation to generation; it can be transmitted from mind to mind by word of mouth; it can be embodied in the intricate formulae of the exact sciences. (Eaton 5)

Eaton's placement of knowledge and meaning within the same axis and the argument about accessibility structures the question of enquiry towards a goal-determined project, assuming that what is to be known is independent of the investigative process. Such categorisation and compartmentalisation, as the poststructuralists have argued, reflect a reduction of sorts, flattening out factors that make it difficult to take a more considered view of the question of knowledge. Closure, in this format, can cancel out not only the modes of reading but become a form of pre-structured agency, compelling critical enquiry to move in an already configured direction. Lyotard's argument about the 'incredulity' towards metanarratives comes to occupy a significant place in such a context; more so as an agency of examination which opens up the question of knowledge and its provisionality as a critical form.

The interrogation of the formulaic approach to knowledge, of which Lyotard's intervention is one example, saw a branching out of the interdisciplinary process where the straitjackets of conventional structures were challenged and re-evaluated. Such a questioning was not brought about as a form of critique directed towards structuralism, but emerged out of the recognition that the idea of looking at knowledge through pre-configured categories would not suffice. Literary and cultural studies, thus, came to acknowledge developments in other disciplines in the wake of poststructuralism as not only significant but also enabling in terms of the insights they offered.

One of the difficulties involved in this process was the marking of the critical space through a registry that could move towards a form of extreme relativism without the argumentative frame being worked out adequately. It appears customary to invoke thinkers such as Derrida, Foucault, or Lyotard in situating the critiquing process and then go on to engage in articulatory planes where the centre is not the key to the question of knowledge. However what is required is not the casual placement of what they set forward, but a critically sustained argumentative frame where consistency would prevail. Poststructuralism is not a designed format ready to be put to use – under its rubric we have an assemblage of critical thought that opens up ways of reading and approaching ideas, concepts and structures, cutting across disciplines. The call for openness and the critical examination of questions such as knowledge, truth and reality facilitate a wider view of the circumstances of engagement with these ideas, which was not quite feasible when structuralism held sway.

REFERENCES

Belsey, Catherine. *Culture and the Real: Theorizing Cultural Criticism*. Routledge, 2005.

Brooks, Cleanth. *The Well-Wrought Urn*. Dennis Dobson, 1949.

Butler, Judith. "Gender in Translation: Beyond Monolingualism". *philoSOPHIA*, vol. 9, no. 1, 2019, pp. 1–25.

De Man, Paul. *The Paul de Man Notebooks*, edited by Martin McQuillan, Edinburgh UP, 2014.

Eaton, Ralph Monroe. *Symbolism and Truth: An Introduction to the Theory of Knowledge*. Dover, 1964.

Foucault, Michel. *Power/Knowledge: Selected Interviews and Other Writings, 1972-1977*. Translated by various, edited by Colin Gordon, Pantheon, 1980.

LaCapra, Dominick. *Writing History, Writing Trauma*. Johns Hopkins UP, 2014.

Lyotard, Jean-François. *The Postmodern Condition: A Report on Knowledge*. Translated by Geoff Bennington and Brian Massumi, U of Minnesota P, 1984.

Nietzsche, Friedrich. *The Will to Power*. Translated by Walter Kaufman and R.J. Hollingdale, Vintage, 1968.

Ricoeur, Paul. *The Conflict of Interpretations*. Translated by various, edited by Don Ihde, Athlone, 1989.

Sass, Louis. "Lacan, Foucault, and the 'Crisis of the Subject': Revisionist Reflections on Phenomenology and Post-structuralism". *Philosophy, Psychiatry, & Psychology*, vol. 21, no. 4, 2014, pp. 325–41.

White, Hayden. "The Value of Narrativity in the Representation of Reality". *Critical Inquiry*, 1980, vol. 7, no. 1, 1980, pp. 5–27.

Young, Robert, editor. *Untying the Text: A Post-Structuralist Reader*. Routledge & Kegan Paul, 1981.

Chapter Six

Poststructuralism Across Disciplines

POSTSTRUCTURALISM BEYOND LITERATURE: PSYCHOANALYSIS, POSTCOLONIALISM AND FEMINISM

The extent to which poststructuralism has marked its space cannot be gauged in terms of interdisciplinarity alone. Modes of reading and engaging with discourses have come to be re-oriented through different registers following the advent of poststructuralism and it's advocating for newer forms in representation. Questions which were located and seen through a binary, structuralist lens have undergone a more critical positioning across disciplinary frontiers. What this has done is open up self-contained academic fields to a more open, analytical process which has impacted not just the subject in the way reading is done, but more significantly, has initiated a crucial interplay of discourses within these fields. It is noteworthy, however, that while the nature of these emerging discourses and critical idioms have gained much from the questioning of structuralist limitations upon a given process of enquiry; each move away from a binary orientation has been a journey that needs to be charted separately. What this implies is that the unsettling of the binaries governing a field such as feminism do not operate through the same register or questioning process when it comes to, say, psychoanalytical theory. This point is a crucial one when it comes to uncovering the fault lines that exist in various critical movements and discursive operations. The umbrella-like expanse of poststructuralism, thus, has come to accommodate a wide range of issues beyond literary and cultural worlds. David R. Howarth places it in context when he states,

> More precisely, poststructuralists have inquired into the construction, form, and role of different social and political identities in various contexts, whether these identities are of a class, ethnic, gender, racial, national, or sexual character. They have also investigated the nature of human subjectivity and its connection to the politics of identity or difference, and they have sought to conceptualize the relationships between structure, agency, and power. At the same time, they have led critical discussions about the problem of ideology, language, and the role of representation more generally in various contexts and social settings. Proponents of poststructuralism have also intervened in central debates about the nature of politics, democracy, and ethics. (1–2)

What initially emerged as a form of critique of structuralism gradually formed into a larger and more expansive bracket which came to extend the theoretical enterprise of critique to disciplines beyond language and society. Why has poststructuralism appealed to thinkers whose areas are so diverse and apparently unrelated? One of the reasons for this is the openness that it grants in approaching and looking at an issue embedded within a discipline, offering not a cul-de-sac but a flexibly-oriented mechanism which keeps space open for articulation and critical engagement. We can look at the ways in which many of the theoretical insights of poststructuralist thought have facilitated the opening up of new frontiers across disciplines.

Poststructuralism and Psychoanalysis

The focus on the unconscious as an area of study and its implications for knowledge relating to the condition of the self, gained prominence with the writings of Sigmund Freud finding space both within the discipline known as psychoanalysis (which he primarily initiated) and beyond it. Subsequently, further questions associated with the unconscious came to be assessed and placed within the broad rubric of psychoanalysis by Carl Gustav Jung, Alfred Alder and Melanie Klein, among others. That the human self was much more than what was evident in the discernible world, even to the subject, came to be recognised and explored through a variety of investigative processes, and often there were contestations relating to the method and nature of the pursuit of such knowledge among psychoanalysts. The Freudian rule book as a methodological toolkit has been remarkably influential in looking at questions of the psyche where the condition of the unconscious as being within the domain of knowability was part of the givens at work. Psychoanalysis has had considerable impact in contesting the idea of a stable self as it shifted the focus from what is seen on the outside to that which remains ordinarily inaccessible. This is the domain of the unconscious. As a current of thought, psychoanalysis has moved along a Freud-led path almost throughout the twentieth century, and the branching out of its many potential configurations have drawn from and moved against the map he laid out for the field. Alternative and rival positions occupied by thinkers such as Gilles Deleuze, Félix Guattari and Fredric Jameson, for instance, have only expanded the field to engage with the discursive questions in formats that bring the self into the centre of the investigation.

The idea that a straight structure would suffice when it came to understanding the world of the unconscious was upset by Freud himself. However, it was Jacques Lacan's sustained re-examination of the nature of the Freudian map that facilitated the emergence of subsequent dynamics in the field. By the time Lacan's *Écrits* consolidated the frontier of his deliberations on the subject, psychoanalysis had been re-oriented from its classic Freudian frame to being seen in its more insistent Lacanian avatar. Lacan built upon the principles laid down by Freud but gave it a contemporary spin by engaging the structuralist thought of Saussure on the one hand and the linguistic skills of Roman Jakobson on the other. In the Lacanian matrix, there was no longer a direct signifier–signified structure, but one where the signified continued to slip out of reach, making the agency of the letter/sign a complex site which held the subject.

It has been argued that Lacan was essentially a structuralist in orientation and his focus on the intelligibility of the grammar of the unconscious places his thought within such a frame. The matter is not as simple to categorise. Lacan was not doing structuralism in the conventional sense. His argumentative model was a very complex design that sought to unravel the workings of the unconscious by proposing an accessible format through which the subject was opened up to psychoanalytic scrutiny. In his 'Seminar' on Edgar Allan Poe's short story 'The Purloined Letter', Lacan presents his formula clearly: 'the unconscious is the discourse of the other' (45). This 'other' is not another individual but that which constitutes what Lacan calls the 'the intersubjective complex' (44) in a subject.

A reading of Lacan as structuralist also locates in the Lacanian analytical model the persistence of a *telos*, which is aimed at and aspired towards as part of the enquiry. Tom Eyers, studying the presence of the structuralist strain in the sixties, comments,

> While it would be a mistake to treat the *Cahiers* as if it were an unproblematic, microcosmic embodiment of the wider formation of structuralism as such, we can at least identify the journal with the particular, problematic conjuncture of Lacanian psychoanalysis and structural Marxism that, for at least a brief period, formed one of the dominant strands of thought immanent to the wider vogue for structural analysis at the time. (46)

Such placements in assessing the nature of the discipline usually situate the work within a pre-set matrix to which the discipline is expected to conform. However, Jacques Lacan's work is not a mirroring of Saussurean structuralism but a complex critical apparatus that significantly shaped the journey of psychoanalytic analysis to argue for a more nuanced and sensitive understanding of the 'agency' of the letter/sign in the human subject. The issues that have persisted in psychoanalytic theory have not found easy resolutions within known structures. Rather, other questions of plurality and the unsettled voices within the realm of the self now occupy this space along with other probing questions. Carolyn Laubender frames the circumstances in which the recurring presence of the self as a site remains relevant, with newer modes of enquiry revisiting the terms through more interesting combinations:

> How, for instance, can one commit to an act of self-narration if one takes seriously the risk of strengthening, not upending,

the ego's tendency toward managerial self-sovereignty? In the wake of psychoanalysis's theory of the split subject, is there a way to write the self that does not confirm the fantasy of conscious, coherent self-knowing? Certainly, these are not new questions for students of twentieth-century critical theory who have cut their teeth on theories of ideology and the protocols of its demystification. (48)

The plurality of selves within the human subject owes much to early work in psychoanalysis more than a century ago. That the connection between knowledge and the subject cannot be a direct road, either in the ambitiously framed Freudian dream-mechanism or under the aegis of a robust subjective agency as formulated by Lacan has often been debated within the field. Lacan's insistence on the accessibility of the self through the deployment of this complex grammar of psychoanalytic truth came under criticism from different quarters. Jacques Derrida was at the forefront of this debate. Derrida argued in his 'The Purveyor of Truth' that Lacan falls into the structuralist trap by suggesting that the self is within the realm of the knowable, however complex the agency of the 'letter' may be, and this constituted a submission to the format of binarism. Derrida was also engaging with the process through which psychoanalysis challenged the very structured sense of the self in another of his essays, 'Freud and the Scene of Writing'. What emerged during the course of these critical engagements in the 1960s and subsequent decades expanded the horizons of the psychoanalytic field from an ambitious determinative format assured of the knowledge of the self by investigation, to a more nuanced engagement with the circumstances of enquiry and the micro aspects that constituted the unconscious in the human subject.

One of the other criticisms directed towards Lacan has been a lack of clarity regarding many of his concepts, something which is not quite as substantial as it is made out to be. If Lacan 'problematised' the mode of enquiry by taking recourse to an argumentative design that asked for an unprecedented grammar to be put to work, it was because he saw the existing critical methodology as being inadequate for a more sustained probing into the nature of the subject. Robert Thomas Kilroy, in reading the critique of Philippe Lacou-Labarthe and Jean-Luc Nancy in their exploration of the dynamics of the psychoanalytic field, argues that the poststructuralist marking in Lacan is borne out both by the queries emanating from within and through the expansion of the critical register beyond it. Kilroy places it thus:

> Lacoue-Labarthe and Nancy appear to isolate what I term the "iconological" core of Lacanian thought, the "word/image parallax" at the root of psychoanalytic theory. It is in this way that their analysis of the Lacanian strategy—when turned symptomatic—goes further than Žižek's and, in doing so, adds a critical "deconstructive" edge to the psychoanalytic method. Through such a shift, psychoanalysis becomes fundamentally Derridean, even if the practice can no longer be called deconstruction. (171)

One of the takeaways of the poststructuralist intervention in different fields, including psychoanalysis, can be seen in the way modes of closure came to be challenged as they served to forfeit the possibility of moving through a more dynamic trajectory in a discipline. Lacan's facilitation of a matrix that sought to explore the move beyond the immediate meaning-making purposefulness of critical enquiry attests to this dimension of poststructuralism. Catherine Liu aptly reads this process when she writes,

> [F]or Lacan, Freud's theories of repetition, had to be amplified by an insistence of the signifier. In order to reinvest language with the radical contingency of the signifier, Lacan undoes the everyday notion of communication by showing that the clinic is a space of exchanges that are irreducible to interpretation on the level of meaning alone. This ostensibly modest lesson, unassailable by mainstream psychoanalysts, has reshaped certain areas of literary and cultural studies. (268–69)

Poststructuralism and Postcolonialism

The examination of the experience of colonialism and the narratives that accompanied it has occupied modern historiography in a variety of ways; one process of which came to be known as postcolonialism. Writers such as Edward Said and Gayatri Chakraborty Spivak, among others, forged a critical space where questions concerning the narrativisation of colonial history and its many attendant discourses found a space for investigation. In his path-breaking book *Orientalism* (1978), Said examined the role played by discursive structures in the formation of the cultural markers that consolidated what came to be known as the 'Orient'; a form of representation through narratives programmed to present a particular point of view. Said's argumentative frame drew upon critical analogies put forward by Michel Foucault where the reading of history was not formatted in a linear pattern but by a more probing process that sought to look at the archaeologies of knowledge production in colonial societies. It was a matter not just of looking at situations as they existed in particular cultures, but more importantly, one that involved the investigation into the circumstances that framed minds through imperceptible designs which were not easy to access or decipher.

While Said has remained extremely influential in shaping the critical processes that come under the rubric of postcolonial thought, there have been interesting movements within the discipline that have considerably invigorated its formative resourcefulness through a reference to possibilities beyond the immediate concerns of a coloniser/colonised binary articulation. When Albert Memmi's book *The Colonizer and the Colonized* was published in 1957 in French (and in English ten years later) it laid down a plan for possible approaches to the experience of colonisation which cut both ways. Memmi was quick to recognise the pitfalls of too direct a structure in assessing the complexities involved in the experience, and said so in his 1965 'Preface' where he sought to place the problem of an either/or categorisation of opposites within an insistent critical frame. Memmi's argumentative frame, however, remained essentially one where the mode of appraisal was conditioned by the need to see the experience from a perspective that was not part of the Western lens.

Postcolonial theory, as a consolidated body of work or as a discipline, has sought to unravel the politics of discourse-making that emerged from the experience of colonialism, and irrespective of the position from which the question is approached, a marker of critique has consistently hovered over its methodological axis. The fact that there have been considerable developments in the current of what constitutes literary theory has had its impact upon thinkers who practice postcolonialism through a variety of critical registers. Commenting on this issue of methodological imperatives impacting critical writing within the discipline, Ato Quayson has made a succinct observation that comes with a rider, acknowledging at the same time how poststructuralism has interpenetrated the field by resisting a direct binary equation as prevalent, for instance, in the example of Albert Memmi. Quayson has sought not only to locate the issue of approach in postcolonial studies in the current moment, but also about how drawing resources and paradigms from other fields affected the focus of a burgeoning field:

> It has to be noted, however, that the trends that were manifested in the study of postcolonial literatures in the 1980s and into the 1990s and 2000s were of a piece with similar reorientations evident in literary studies more generally, which from at least the early 1980s had been heavily impacted by the poststructuralist and neo-formalist approaches of Michel Foucault, Jacques Lacan, Pierre Bourdieu, and Mikhail Bakhtin. For me, however, the source of constant regret was the progressive, one might say almost decisive, retreat from the rigorous reading of literature that came to pass under the rubric of postcolonial literary criticism. Reading literature for its literariness was regarded as almost an admission of moral deficiency. (Quayson 300)

In his book *Tragedy and Postcolonial Literature* (2021) Quayson offers a critically engaging perspective on the way classical tropes continue to invigorate our understanding of social realities through connectives that can be identified with literature through the ages. In this context, the question of method becomes significant. He argues that method or approach cannot be divorced from poststructuralist interventions that have come to be part of the critical discourses that engage with revisiting colonial history. As recent developments in postcolonial studies have shown, questions has moved beyond the colony and the site, unlike in works by critics like Memmi who sought to locate the critical exegesis in such spaces, with much more intricate circumstances finding space in postcolonial arguments on space, identity and society. The example of Natalie Diaz's *Postcolonial Love Poem* (2021) and the challenges it brings to the reader as well as the critic can serve as a case in point. A binarily structured approach to the idea of colonial experience will not serve a purpose here. Reviewing the book, Deborah A. Miranda writes of the complexities involved in assessing such a text: '"Postcolonial" is a word that confusingly doesn't, and does, apply to life in today's Native America: we are simultaneously alive after the initial blow of colonization and yet still subject to a barrage of colonizing injustices and microaggressions that impact our daily lives, often in violent ways' (Miranda 94). Fractures within contemporary spaces challenge the idea of the postcolonial, the reading of which cannot be accommodated within the frames that served in the initial critiques of colonial experience. Memmi, for instance, formulates a structurally-driven position which would not work in the context Diaz is writing her poems in. Not only has content seen a drastic makeover, we also see a more elastic, nuanced and critically alert approach to contemporary experience. Memmi looks at the coloniser and places the figure thus: 'It is neither pure jealousy nor perverseness which draws him irresistibly toward supreme temptation, but rather that inner inevitability or usurpation – moral and physical suppression of the usurped' (Memmi 53). Homi K. Bhabha, for instance, moves beyond the position postulated by earlier critical thinkers such as Memmi, especially when it comes to reading 'a discursive event' (Bhabha 34), by which he refers to the manner in which the political subject is engaged with or located in culture. Bhabha's interventions in postcolonial theory have drawn upon the evolving dynamics of the conceptual paradigm within the field: a process which lays bare the limitations of a binary orientation in engaging with issues in colonial discourse. It is interesting to see the intersections of convergence across postcolonial theory and poststructuralist thought where cross-fertilisation of concepts, ideas and reading strategies present the fluidity that informs the process of criticism today.

In such a context, it is evident that concepts have also undergone change; nuances of reading and explication being contextualised with the changed nature of experiential combinations where structures are being challenged and re-oriented. The flux in contemporary experience with subjects such as racism and migrancy, to name two, constantly altering the thought and receptive apparatus of both lay people and critical articulators calls for a more flexibly oriented framework, especially when it comes to conceptualisation and placement. What would serve in a particular social or political context does not quite work the same way in another context which may be slightly altered due to locally embedded circumstances. What this does, in effect, is to invalidate the force of a critical concept if used as an umbrella term, something the poststructuralist argumentative process has facilitated. Eli Park Sorensen lays out this dilemma and the emerging critical fluidity with reference to what poststructuralism can find itself being invested in when a concept such as Benedict Anderson's 'imagined communities' is taken up for appraisal:

> As poststructuralist-oriented postcolonial scholars have been eager to point out, Anderson's concept of imagined communities relies on a discourse of language, which thus lends itself to deconstructive strategies. However, this deconstructive procedure precisely misses the essential point of Anderson's definition: that the latter's concept is no longer a sign but is experienced as reality itself. And it is precisely due to this feeling—the national as natural, real, and not as a sign or something constructed or artificial—that individuals begin to imagine and dream beyond the now secure notion of the collective; ... When the concept of reality is no longer understood or experienced as a concept, an idea, a fiction, but reality as such ... the performative-political force of realism becomes largely anachronistic. (Sorensen 118)

Sorensen is not mapping out a field of contestation, but referring to the changed focus in critical discourse where a static approach to questions of nation and identity can backtrack an argument relating to such a crucial term as reality. Placed within the matrix of postcolonialism, reality becomes a site and configuration for which closed frames will not suffice.

Postcolonial critics are increasingly facing problems of contradiction that have percolated to occupy the critical space where questions of location and identity, along with the politics of seeing, emerge as inevitabilities that cannot be shied away from. That the subject is much more complex than what the theoretical apparatus is able to dissect is a recognition that calls for greater flexibility and a more cautionary approach, as stated clearly here by Elleke Boehmer:

> Aggravating the situation further is the fact that postcolonial critics, many of them located in the west, have found themselves in the contradictory situation of imposing their interpretative frameworks of otherness and difference from above and outside the postcolonial cultures and texts they are describing, thus operating in effect as did colonial systems of knowledge, its oppressive and hegemonic ways. In this sense, postcolonial critique is not only homogenizing and universalizing in its heuristic effects, it is also depoliticizing, even deradicalizing, its relation to the resistance it reads and for which it wishes to enlist respect. (309)

Poststructuralism has impacted areas of study such as postcolonialism not merely through an offering of a critical apparatus. As Boehmer points out above, reading methods within a discipline cannot be inattentive to the fault lines that drive wedges even in positions that are alert to self-scrutiny. For a reading position not to consolidate as a given within a field, the manoeuvrability of the critical arguments ought to be such that questions of identity or eminence cannot be dislodged without incapacitating its effectiveness. Poststructuralism facilitates those critical underpinnings within disciplines that enable them to continuously reassess the parameters of engagement, something we can see when it comes to postcolonialism.

Poststructuralism and Feminism

The landmark publication of Simone de Beauvoir's *The Second Sex* in 1949 opened up the field of Gender Studies, the critical examination of the divide challenging the 'natural' placement of women after men in the hierarchical scale. It thus sought to dismantle the structure of the opposition between man and woman, where the idea of inferiority was exposed as a cultural matrix that had become consolidated with usage and the unquestioning acceptance of it as reality. While Beauvoir's forceful argumentative framework opened up space for the reassessment of the critical environment pertaining to the how the gender equation was viewed, her position remained an essentialist one, devised to call for the dissolution of the inequality structure that existed in public discourse. By the 1960s however, there was considerable development in the space that came to be known as feminism which was accentuated by the critical interventions of thinkers such as Luce Irigaray, Hélène Cixous and Julia Kristeva. The complications involved in a binary orchestration of the gender question came to be increasingly felt in circles of feminist thought and the search for a more elastic space became persistent in feminist theory.

When Julia Kristeva published her essay 'Word, Dialogue and the Novel' – which was one of the earliest assessments of the impact and importance of Mikhail Bakhtin in the non-Russian critical space – she was moving beyond one of the criticisms of the dialogic frame proposed by the Russian thinker, which was that Bakhtin was not sensitive to the voice of women. What Kristeva was doing was to envision a complete methodological shift in orientation which would have remarkable implications for critical theory, including feminism. It called for, Kristeva argued, a 'break' from the discursive patterns that had been serving as engagements in critical space, a break from the mode of structuring things in the way they are placed and taken up for evaluation. In this essay, Kristeva examines the broader implications of challenging set notions, thereby moving towards an argumentative framework where fixed conditions and taken-for-granted assumptions cannot hold sway. She writes, 'Carnivalesque discourse breaks through the laws of a language censored by grammar and semantics and, at the same time, is a social and political protest. There is no equivalence, but rather, identity between challenging official linguistic codes and challenging official law' (Kristeva 36).

The French feminists made interesting critical interventions that have now been situated as part of the Second Wave, the movement branching across diverse spaces to look at and accommodate issues which a more structuralist orientation could not adequately address. Kristeva's work, again, has been the subject of contestation by critics such as Judith Butler, who see in the framing a sense of foreclosure that does not offer sufficient space for engagement with hitherto unclaimed spaces of identity through the gender lens. In an essay titled 'The Body Politics of Julia Kristeva', Butler takes issue with some of Kristeva's contentions and her configuration of a materialist grounding for the assessment of language and gender identity, arguing that it does not make space for many orientations that move beyond a structured identity frame.

> The maternal body in its originary signification is considered by Kristeva to be prior to signification itself; hence, it becomes impossible within her framework to consider the maternal itself as a signification, open to cultural variability. Her argument makes clear that maternal drives constitute those primary processes that language invariably represses or sublimates. But perhaps her argument could be recast within an even more encompassing framework: what cultural configuration of language, indeed, of discourse, generates the trope of a pre-discursive libidinal multiplicity, and for what purposes? (Butler 115)

What such a debate offers is fascinating for the critical vista, facilitated by the interventions of poststructuralist thought from which both Kristeva and Butler have emerged. It is significant that no argumentative position sees itself as something that requires to be consolidated to make its point within the subject-frame. That Kristeva and Butler debate through the aegis of gender as a critical space speaks for the highly contested realm that feminism has become, especially in terms of the inward-looking exercises ongoing within the discipline. By the time the Second Wave had been consolidated into a substantial body of work and became earmarked as a movement, its ideas and genealogies branched into different directions involving questions beyond the binary male/female gender equation. This process did not entail the disruption of the feminist thinking that had emerged as a tradition, but its eventualities came to be contested through a variety of critical registers. Hélène Cixous's discursive reading of the act of writing is an eye-opener: 'What I can write is already written, it is no longer of interest. I always head towards the most frightening. This is what makes writing thrilling but painful. I write towards what I flee. I dream about it. It is always a *jardin d'Essai*, but it is an infernal, expelling garden' (Cixous and Derrida 9). If writing and reading are not set exercises, they mark out a form of flexibility that overrides the essentialism at the core of conventional enquiry in classical feminism.

What such developments suggest is that the field of feminism is no longer constrained by the emphasis on a quest for 'equality', but is engaged with areas that consider the challenging of existing formats and the seeking of new knowledge frontiers as priorities within the discipline. Poststructuralist interventions in feminist thought have facilitated a critical reading of issues that show a move towards the reorientation of settled terminologies within the discipline itself. Whether we situate thinkers such as Cixous and Irigaray as feminists or philosophers is another matter, but the fact that the thinking within the fold has sought to articulate the circumstances of reading outside the conditioned formats of classical feminism shows the cultivation of possibilities that have come a long way from the structures governing questions such as equality and rights alone. Both domestic and public spaces situate the different genders (not just women) in a variety of contexts, which contemporary feminism has taken up the cudgel for. A closed form of a binary-driven feminist argumentative frame would not suffice to address questions that need to be looked at from a more sustainable critical environment.

The insights of poststructuralist thought have not come to feminism without being subjected to scrutiny. What we find in the course of these discourses finding space within feminism is a fascinating play of argumentation that is significantly directed towards both self-critique and an outward appraisal of the parameters that are used for the purposes of enquiry. Structured straitjackets can be difficult to negotiate within a discipline, which thinkers like Monique Wittig have cautioned about; a process that requires not only the intervention of revisionist reading but also a more engaging lens for new pathways to be charted and brought into the public sphere. For such a process to be initiated, critical discourses have to find space for articulation and statement which is not easy. Wittig, in the following example, talks about the problems of pre-set determination within feminist formats which resist any departure that would require flexibility on the part of fixed structures. Referring to the process of consolidation that has controlled the binary structuring of thought and its impact on feminist thought, Wittig writes,

> The perenniality of the sexes and the perenniality of slaves and masters proceed from the same belief, and, as there are no slaves without masters, there are no women without men. The ideology of sexual difference functions as censorship in our culture by masking, on the ground of nature, the social opposition between men and women. Masculine/feminine, male/female are the categories which serve to conceal the fact that social differences always belong to an economic, political, ideological order. . . . the divisions are abstracted and turned into concepts by the masters, and later on by the slaves when they rebel and start to struggle. The masters explain and justify the established divisions as a result of natural differences. The slaves, when they rebel and start to struggle, read social oppositions into the so-called natural differences. (Wittig 2)

Wittig goes on to dismantle the structured model through which society has embedded the notion of heterosexuality as a normative imperative, one that classical feminism takes on in its contestation of the critical space where discourses regarding the 'women question' are placed and negotiated. Wittig's remarkably sustained breakthrough is a move that demands a complete upheaval of settled binaries where feminist thought had fought battles against gender bias. That the very ambit of this contestation was configured to submit to the structure of the man/woman design was something that Wittig red-flagged vociferously. What it brought about is a challenge to the feminist formatting of priorities where the very idea of culture was seen to have been programmed to further the idea of heterosexual normativity. This was a major step forward in feminist studies as it struck at the edifice of a structured design where any query would substantially result in only the consolidation of the purpose being contested. In the same essay, Wittig argues,

> For the category of sex is a totalitarian one, which to prove true has its inquisitions, its courts, its tribunals, its body of

laws, its terrors, its tortures, its mutilations, its executions, its police. It shapes the mind as well as the body since it controls all mental production. . . . This is why we must destroy it and start thinking beyond it if we want to start thinking at all, as we must destroy the sexes as a sociological reality if we want to start to exist. (8)

As pointed as it is pertinent, Wittig strikes at the base of the structuralist orientation that had served the feminist discursive mechanism from Woolf and Beauvoir to those who championed for the equal rights of women. In such rigid pursuits lay the trappings of a systematic enhancement of the philosophy of a normative structure which Wittig sought to overhaul and challenge.

The nature of the attack on the forms of engagement within settled feminist discourses shows the questioning of structured thought, and its limitations are thus laid bare in a reappraisal of the critical scene within the discipline. In contemporary critical discourse the diversification of areas of enquiry are no longer confined to the normativity of the heterosexual structure but address micro and previously marginally placed circumstances including those involving colour and ethnic situations. Such movements beyond the settled materiality of structured discourses have shed light upon areas where poststructuralist interventions in other fields have served as examples of figuring out ways of enquiry and critical analysis.

REFERENCES

Boehmer, Elleke. "Revisiting Resistance: Postcolonial Practice and the Antecedents of Theory". *The Oxford Handbook of Postcolonial Studies*, edited by Graham Huggan, Oxford UP, 2013, pp. 307–23.

Butler, Judith. "The Body Politics of Julia Kristeva", *Hypatia*, vol. 3, no. 3, 1989, pp. 104–18.

Derrida, Jacques and Hélène Cixous. "From the Word to Life: A Dialogue between Jacques Derrida and Hélène Cixous". Interviewed by Aliette Armel and translated by Ashley Thompson, *New Literary History*, vol. 37, no. 1, 2006, pp. 1–13.

Eyers, Tom. "Psychoanalytic Structuralism in the *Cahiers Pour L'Analyse*", *Angelaki*, vol. 18 no. 2, 2013, pp. 45–60.

Howarth, David R. *Poststructuralism and After: Structure, Subjectivity and Power.* Palgrave, 2013.

Kilroy, Robert Thomas. "Lacan through Lacoue-Labarthe and Nancy: From 'Modernist Myths' to Modernism as Myth", *L'Esprit Créateur*, vol. 57, no. 4, 2017, pp. 160–73.

Kristeva, Julia. *The Julia Kristeva Reader*, edited by Toril Moi, Columbia UP, 1986.

Lacan, Jacques. "Seminar on 'The Purloined Letter'". Translated by Jeffrey Mehlman, *Yale French Studies*, no. 48, 1972, pp. 39–72.

Laubender, Carolyn. "Speak for Your Self: Psychoanalysis, Autotheory, and The Plural Self", *Arizona Quarterly*, vol. 76, no. 1, 2020, pp. 39–64.

Liu, Catherine. "Lacan's Afterlife: Jacques Lacan meets Andy Warhol". *The Cambridge Companion to Lacan*, edited by Jean-Michael Rabaté, Cambridge UP, 2003, pp. 253–71.

Memmi, Albert. *The Colonizer and the Colonized.* Translated by Howard Greenfield, Beacon Press, 1967.

Miranda, Deborah A. "Review of *Postcolonial Love Poem* by Natalie Diaz", *Western American Literature*, vol. 56, no. 1, 2021, pp. 93–96.

Quayson, Ato. *Tragedy and Postcolonial Literature.* Cambridge UP, 2021.

Sorensen, Eli Park. *Postcolonial Realism and the Concept of the Political.* Routledge, 2021.

Wittig, Monique. *The Straight Mind and Other Essays.* Beacon Press, 1992.

Glossary of Select Terms

Aporia: a Greek term that describes an irresolvable internal contradiction or logical disjunction in a text, argument, or theory. Its primary use as a figure of speech was as a site that presented debaters with the objective of deliberating on how to resolve that which eluded fixity. Appropriated into the scheme of locating the condition of play, aporia is one of the terms through which deconstruction's methodology can be approached. See Chapter 2 for a detailed discussion.

Différance: a term coined by Derrida to refer to the conjunction of difference and deferment – attributes which are at work (or rather, play) within a structure, which indicates that a settled, confirmed meaning cannot be appropriated from within a given frame of reference. See Chapter 2 for a detailed discussion.

Dissemination: the process of dispersion that breaks out from within the text to thwart any central core from manifesting meaning conclusively. While the text has a structure framing it, the playfulness that makes it a site of dynamic movement does not permit it to coalesce, so much so that the exercise of meaning-making has to deal with a process of constant movement. Since there is dispersal, there is no possibility of any settled meaning being accessible at a given time. See Chapter 2 for a detailed discussion.

Grammatology: refers to the act and process of writing. In deconstruction, and the way in which Derrida locates the term for the purposes of examining its situation in a binary formation where 'speech' is its other, grammatology is seen not in terms of its confinement within a fixed axis but as an iterative condition. Derrida's focus directs us to the limitations of relying on a mode of access which does not permit movement beyond the speech/writing dualism. See Chapter 2 for a detailed discussion.

Indeterminacy: in deconstruction implies that 'meaning' is not absolutely fixed within the system of signs. Indeterminacy is not the same as the difference in interpretation of texts. It involves the recognition that because of the inherent play within the realm of signification, the signifier–signified relationship does not lead to determined or conclusive meaning. This view has implications for the self-contained limits of the sign as proposed by Saussure because even though the sign is seen to be arbitrary, once the signification process is complete meaning is believed to be made. Deconstruction and other poststructuralist reading positions open up the inconsistencies in the Saussurean framework by arguing that indeterminacy is an inherent aspect of the system of signs. Indeterminacy is evident in the recognition that play is inevitably triggered when the structure becomes operational.

Also see: **aporia, play**

Logocentrism: a term coined by German philosopher Ludwig Klages in the early 1900s referring to the tradition of Western science and philosophy that regards words and language as a fundamental expression of an external reality. A crucial term in deconstruction, Derrida points out that the reasoning behind the assumption that the word or *logos* is central to the thought-making process is fraught with fault lines that must be examined. See Chapter 2 for a detailed discussion.

Metanarrative: refers to a grand totalising process which has as its goal something that is complete in itself. Usually, a narrative is taken to be about something, and the objective of narration is understood as being about telling and showing a singular subject. A metanarrative is an overarching narrative which seeks to explain/narrate an extensive field such as religion or history. Poststructuralists disavow such grand and totalising narrative frameworks which seek to explain a field comprehensively. The French thinker Lyotard uses the term 'incredulity' to argue that the efficacy of grand narratives to sustain systems of thought has been challenged in contemporary critical theory as fixity or determinacy cannot be assured in the meaning-making process.

Also see: **totalisation**

Play: in deconstruction, refers to the slippery nature of the meaning-making process within a system of signs. In the Saussurean scheme of the sign, the relationship between the signifier and the signified is a settled one, and when they are coordinated, signification takes place. Derrida argues that signifiers lead to other signifiers and the belief that complete or total meaning can be achieved is not possible. When we look at the signification process we can see within it 'aporetic' spaces which cannot be resolved, but remain indeterminate. When a person responds by saying 'What's the difference?' to the query about their choice of tea or coffee, the semiologically controlled information-seeking exercise is simultaneously layered with the implication that 'coffee and tea are not different for them in the given context'. In such an orientation difference *is* sameness or no difference at all. The centre of the sign, thus, is subject to play because even as 'difference' is a signifier here, the signified remains indeterminate. It does not mean that one meaning is to be prioritised over another; it does not imply an either/or formulation. It involves the coexistence of 'both/and' which is fluid and not contained within limited choices. In effect, there is a deferral of total meaning which resists the closure of the signification process.

Also see: **aporia, différance, supplementarity, totalisation**

Supplementarity: A crucial term in Derrida's critical lexicon, the term refers to that element which extends the potential of the 'totalised' framework of any given signification process. In his essay, 'Structure, Sign, and Play in the Discourse of the Human Sciences' Derrida puts forward the argument that what seems to be 'contained' or 'totalized' *does not* remain there but is enhanced by its supplement. For instance, when we look at something as dynamic as culture, newly incorporated facets are drawn into its fabric which impacts its existing view. Prior to any intervention in the form of the 'new' or 'additional' element into the totalised fabric, the supplement stands outside its frame. We can take the example of the concept of a story, which is continuously revised with the incorporation of *additional* or *supplementary* elements with time and context. This elasticity is part of any concept which seems to be self-operational prior to the supplement's entry into its domain. An element's entry into a concept's domain testifies to its supplementary status, which works to enhance and re-ordinate the character of the concept. This process is also connected to the

Glossary of Select Terms 111

idea of play which is manifested in the resistance to totalisation that takes place within the realm of signification.

Also see: **aporia, play, totalisation**

Totalisation: implies the understanding that meaning is contained within the signification system. In other words, when something is signified it is taken to be complete or total. However, the potential of a signifier to refer to elements beyond that which is either apparent or closed remains within the significatory realm. Poststructuralists argue that closure with respect to meaning is untenable as the resistance to totalisation comes from within the system of signs. In this view, meaning that emerges from a structure can be contextual or provisional, but not total.

Undecidability: When the meaning from a structure or a concept cannot be accessed in a finalised form because the inherent registers lead to multiple possibilities, then it can be said that the condition reflects undecidability. Conceptually, the possibility of arriving at meaning is a sign of closure, for it is that which is done after other possibilities have given way to what emerges as a feasible situation in relation to the concept in question. But this is not so simply organised or structured such that meaning can be directly drawn out in an absolute sense. As the equation of concept–knowledge is not settled decisively, the structure remains inconclusive in terms of the 'meaning' it generates, which is in effect provisional. Undecidability is the sign and indication of the structure being open, and not closed. See Chapter 2 for a detailed discussion.

Suggested Reading

Baross, Zsuzsa. *Posthumously: For Jacques Derrida*. Sussex Academic P, 2011.

Berggren, Kalle. "Sticky Masculinity: Post-structuralism, Phenomenology and Subjectivity in Critical Studies on Men", *Men and Masculinities*, vol. 17, no. 3, pp. 231–52.

Bryla, Martyna. "Postdependent Eastern Europe: Critical Avenues and Literary Representations", *Ariel: A Review of International English Literature*, vol. 52, no. 2, 2021, pp. 163–90.

Derrida, Jacques. *Acts of Religion*, edited by Gil Anidjar, Routledge, 2002.

---. *Basic Writings*, edited by Barry Stocker, Routledge, 2007.

---. *Of Grammatology*. Translated by Gayatri Chakravorty Spivak, Johns Hopkins UP, 1976.

---. *Points...: Interviews, 1974–1994*. Translated by Peggy Kamuf, edited by Elizabeth Weber, Stanford UP, 1995.

---. *Spectres of Marx*. Translated by Peggy Kamuf, Routledge, 2006.

---. *Writing and Difference*. Translated and edited by Alan Bass, Routledge, 2001.

Critchley, Simon. *The Ethics of Deconstruction*, 3rd ed., Edinburgh UP, 2014.

Culler, Jonathan. *On Deconstruction*. Routledge, 1982.

Foucault, Michel. "Madness, the Absence of Work". Translated by Peter Stastny and Deniz Şengel, *Critical Inquiry*, vol. 21, no. 2, 1995, pp. 290–98.

---. *Power/Knowledge: Selected Interviews and Other Writings, 1972-1977*. Translated by various, edited by Colin Gordon, Pantheon, 1980

---. *The Order of Things*. Translated by A.M. Sheridan, Routledge, 2002.

Goodfield, Eric. "Postmodern Paper Tiger: Lyotard, Baudrillard, and the Contemporary Politics of Poststructuralist Subversion", *Cultural Politics*, vol. 16, no. 2, 2020, pp. 233–52.

Grassby, Richard. "Material Culture and Cultural History", *Journal of Interdisciplinary History*, vol. 35, no. 4, 2005, pp. 591–603.

Gunkel, David J. *Deconstruction*. MIT P, 2021.

Irzik, Sibel. *Deconstruction and the Politics of Criticism*. Routledge, 2016.

Kilroy, Robert Thomas. "Lacan through Lacoue-Labarthe and Nancy: From 'Modernist Myths' to Modernism as Myth", *L'Esprit Créateur*, vol. 57, no. 4, 2017, pp. 160–73.

Kristeva, Julia. *The Julia Kristeva Reader*, edited by Toril Moi, Columbia UP, 1986.

Levi-Strauss, Claude. *Structural Anthropology*. Translated by Claire Jacobson and Brooke Grundfest Schoepf, Basic Books, 1963.

---. *Structural Anthropology Zero*. Translated by Ninon Vinsonneau and Jonathan Magidoff, edited by Vincent Debaene, Polity, 2022.

Loesberg, Jonathan. *Aestheticism and Deconstruction: Pater, Derrida, and de Man*. Princeton UP, 1991.

Naas, Michael. *Taking on the Tradition: Jacques Derrida and the Legacies of Deconstruction*. Stanford UP, 2002

Pluth, Ed. *Signifiers and Acts: Freedom in Lacan's Theory of the Subject*. SUNY P, 2007.

Proudfit, Scott. "Reunion, Complication, Refraction, and Translation: How Postcolonialism and Post-Structuralism Mark *Bengal Tiger at the Baghdad Zoo*", *Modern Drama*, vol. 60, no. 4, 2017, pp. 480–500.

Saussure, Ferdinand de. *Course in General Linguistics*. Translated by Wade Baskin, Philosophical Library, 1959.

Stawarska, Beata. *Saussure's Linguistics, Structuralism, and Phenomenology: The Course in General Linguistics after a Century*, Palgrave Macmillan, 2020.

Sturrock, John. *Structuralism*, Blackwell, 2003.

Wills, David. *Matchbook: Essays in Deconstruction*. Stanford UP, 2005.

Other books in the series

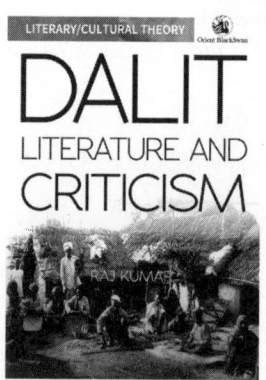

For more information, visit www.orientblackswan.com

Other books in the series

For more information, visit www.orientblackswan.com

Other books in the series

For more information, visit www.orientblackswan.com